Up the Boohai Shooting Pukakas

A DICTIONARY OF
KIWI
SLANG

By David McGill

Mills Publications

Dedicated to Brett,
who taught me Kiwi slang in London
and will recognise
his own contributions herein.

Cover illustration by Tom Scott

First publication 1988
Reprinted 1988, 1989 (twice), 1990 (twice), 1993, 1995
MILLS PUBLICATIONS
P.O. BOX 30-818
Lower Hutt, New Zealand

ISBN 0-908722-35-4 (Limp Bound)

Typeset by Sabagraphics, Christchurch
Edited by Anna Rogers
Design and production by Lindsay Cuthbertson
Printed in Hong Kong through Bookprint Consultants, Wellington

Introduction

This is the first wide-ranging collection of Kiwi slang and informal language since Sidney J. Baker's *New Zealand Slang, A Dictionary of Colloquialisms*, published by Whitcombe and Tombs in Christchurch, 1941. Like many other such collections elsewhere, this effort slings its net over most means of common metaphorical expression, including catchphrases, colloquialisms or conversational usage, exclamations, words creeping out of the subcultures or special interests of gambling, horse racing, boozing, cooking, armed forces, competitive sports, tramping, street talk, regional oddities and nicknames, religious rivalries, Maori/Pakeha interaction, obsolete words — everything that adds up to a collection of Kiwi usage. A new word is perhaps needed for a collection that aims to present the New Zealand word experience. *Oxford English Dictionary Supplement* editor and New Zealander Robert Burchfield has referred to 'New Zealandisms'. No? Kiwiana?

Like most collections of slang and informal language, this one owes an enormous debt to Eric Partridge, the great New Zealander without peer as a collector of international English slang. This effort is perhaps most indebted to him for what it left out. Unlike most other such books, this one has tried to include only what is characteristic of this country, or of predominantly Kiwi usage. Other dictionaries use all the words circulating within their linguistic borders, whether they be from England, Ireland, Scotland, Wales, the United States, Australia or Canada. This collection does not include common usage such as 'Blighty' once was, because that is of British military origin — or 'jacksy', which one Australian collection identifies as New Zealand, but which Partridge puts the kibosh on, giving it as army and navy originally. Much as one might like to include a catchphrase such as somebody 'wouldn't know his arse from a hole in the ground', Partridge, in his *A Dictionary of Catch Phrases*, sources it to Canada.

The biggest barrier to separating out specifically local usage is the Australians. Politically we almost joined them a century ago, and at present our businessfolk want to join them economically. Linguistically, we have always been pretty unified. The differences (or 'deeferences', as an Australian would say) are disappearing so fast — owing to the Three Triumphant Ts of trade, telly and travel — that this may be the last good chance to pin down a good portion of Kiwiana.

Despite such an intention, however, much of this book has to recognise the Australian connection. While words such as 'daks' and 'norks' are omitted because they come from Australian brandnames, others such as 'duckshove' undoubtedly originate there, but have crossed the Tasman so comprehensively that they are part of our usage too, and these are identified at the end of the entry as 'ANZ', short for Australia New Zealand, but with the origin emphasised. Where the origin is not so clear but the word is common in both countries, I end the entry 'NZA'. Where the word originated and generally stayed here, I have not marked it.

My principal personal debt is to Harry Orsman, who also did not mark words that are New Zealand in his *Heinemann New Zealand Dictionary*, on the grounds that this is what his dictionary is about. He is a most enthusiastic Kiwi joker, proud to share the common pronunciation 'New Zilland', and a delighter in our colloquial expressions. We have exchanged Kiwi phrases over a few beers from time to time, and he was kind enough to suggest me for this book. Not only did he usher a journalistic poacher into his lexicographers' preserve, but he was also kind enough to cast a sharp eye over my first draft. I have jibbed at some of his academic constraints, on the grounds that we need everything we have in the continued development of our national identity.

To further complicate the Australian connection, I am also indebted to Kiwi lexicographers who set up shop there after Baker, particularly George Turner for *The English Language in Australia and New Zealand* (Longmans, 1966). Behind them all is Partridge with his *A Dictionary of Slang and Unconventional English*, currently in its eighth edition from Routledge, and that other great New Zealand lexicographer, Robert Burchfield, the general editor of the *Oxford English Dictionary Supplement*, its fourth and last volume published in 1986. Burchfield has also edited *The New Zealand Pocket Oxford Dictionary*, while *The New Collins Concise English Dictionary New Zealand Edition* is edited by Ian A. Gordon who, as Harry Orsman's professor of English at Victoria University of Wellington, set him off on his professional lifetime of collecting New Zealand English. I was a student of both Professor Gordon and Harry Orsman, so there is no escaping this tight series of connections.

In general, however, you would not find, nor would you expect to find, the entries in this book in the formal dictionaries from Oxford, Collins, Macquarie and such. Orsman's Heinemann defines slang as 'the form of a language consisting of words in popular, current, informal use, as distinct from the formal, established language'. Slang is social and alive and not usually polite.

Slang is the cutting edge of language. Slang emerges as society changes, and tends to be thickest where change is most apparent, as in pioneering periods, among the movers and shakers, the self-starters, the outcasts and the outlaws, the people pushed together with the common aim of pushing ahead. After the land is broken in, the slang habit moves into other active areas, such as sport and the underworld of villains and gamblers, among men at war and men and women at work.

In this collection the entry 'late C19' (for the 19th century) is a common one. As the 1898 *Websters Dictionary* noted: 'The latest great expansion of the English stock [i.e. language] has been in Australia, Tasmania, and New Zealand, where new conditions of society have produced a multitude of new verbal usages.' Some of them are included.

Turner, in his book on Australian and New Zealand language, observes: 'So far as language is concerned, the term Australasian could well be revived to refer to a single variety of English with two major subdivisions.' This may not be acceptable to all New Zealanders, but there is no word not starting with 'A' that does the job. I have sometimes used 'antipodean' and mostly avoided 'Australasian' as inappropriate to this task, nowhere more so than in our singular adaptation of Maori words. Harry Orsman has commented on the criticism he encountered for including words and phrases that may be offensive to Maori people, such as 'Maori PT'. He has said that is not his concern; his job is to record, note if offensive, but not to pass judgement on usage. This collection takes the same view, and indeed probably extends this area, for slang and informal language is, by its very nature, often vulgar and potentially offensive to some. Much slang never graduates to an entry in a formal dictionary, so if it finds no home in a collection such as this, it is lost to recorded history.

I have many home-grown contributors to thank, some of whom are quoted in the text. Jim and Jean Henderson were a wonderful source of mostly World War II slang and catchphrases. The period just after 1945 has been superbly recorded by Gordon Slatter in his two novels, *A Gun in My Hand* (1959) and *The Pagan Game* (1968); the period before 1939 by Stevan Eldred-Grigg in his *Oracles and Miracles* (1987). My brothers-in-law, Major Patrick McDonald and Captain Richard McDonald, have been gun on current Kiwi army slang, while another brother-in-law, Michael McDonald, and his sister Ginette, my dear wife, have also dobbed in the Kiwiana of their extra Kiwi lass, Lyn of Tawa.

I thank Burton Silver for his eclectic contributions, Brian Sergent for some cracker catchphrases and gambling terms, Alex Veysey for horse racing and sporting terms, Alison Gray for teenage chat, Jim and Mary Barr for the way teenagers used to slang it, Judith Fyfe and Hugo Manson for early access to the way some very senior citizens spoke for the New Zealand Oral History record, Joy and Lloyd Shepard for grouse rural chatter, a lot of those fast disappearing guards for talking me through New Zealand by rail a few years ago, those Wellington folk who talked to me about the old town and those folk who talked ghost towns to me a decade ago. Tom Ward, Tom Scott and Roger Hall are others I thank for their contributions. Last and most, I thank my father for his contributed list and for passing on his love of books and language.

It is partly obvious from listed quotes, but a number of writers and compilers were goldmines of informal language, notably Frank S. Anthony with his *Me and Gus* stories; Barry Crump, particularly for *Hang on a Minute, Mate*; Edward Jerningham Wakefield for *Adventure in New Zealand*; John A. Lee, particularly for *Shiner Slattery*; Brian Sutton-Smith, particularly for *The Games of New Zealand Children* (University of California Press, 1959), available from the Education Department; Ruth Mason's two studies in the Tararua tramping magazine annuals for 1958 and 1959; L.G.D. Acland's *The Early Canterbury Runs* (Whitcombe and Tombs, 1951); A.S. Thomson's *History of New Zealand* (1859); Arnold Wall's *New Zealand English* (1938); Charles Money's *Knocking About in New Zealand* (1871); C.R. Thatcher's *Canterbury Songster* (1862); Louis S. Leland Jr.'s *A Personal Kiwi-Yankee Dictionary* (1980); E.E. Morris' *Austral-English, A Dictionary of Australasian Words* (1898); the delightful Macquarie Dictionary of Australian Colloquialisms, *Aussie Talk* (1984), whose direct or indirect contributors include Harry Orsman and Dr Bill Ramson, another New Zealander and a founding editor of the *Macquarie Dictionary*; the brief but bountiful J.A.W. Bennett essay 'English As It Is Spoken in New Zealand', published in *English Transported* (Australian National University Press, Canberra, 1970); lastly, perhaps the first and certainly one of our best recorders of lingo on the farm and in the woolshed, Lady Barker's *Station Life in New Zealand* (1870).

Beside, behind and even beyond many of these primary sources feature the male Ocker outpourings of Bazza McKenzie and Sir Les

Patterson, for whom Barry Humphries takes the cake and this author's admiration, tinged with relief that Barry was not born here, for how could one possibly separate the Humphries inventions from the dinkum Australian oil?

As well as getting in behind yet another of my efforts, editor Anna Rogers dobbed in a few doozies.

The end of this beginning should pay tribute to Eric Partridge. In *Slang, Yesterday and Today* he wrote appreciatively of slang's 'force and picturesqueness, its richness and variety', qualities he attributed partly to the exhilarating and often romantic occupation of countries, partly to intrepid and resourceful settlers. Most appropriate, perhaps, is his first entry on slang in his magnum opus *Dictionary of Slang and Unconventional English*: 'The special vocabulary of low, illiterate, or disreputable persons: 1756.' Actually, that is just the start . . .

Abbreviations

aka also known as
ANZ Australia New Zealand
Brit. British
c/p catchphrase
NZA New Zealand Australia
obs. obsolete
phr. phrase
post-war after World War II
ref. reference
US United States of America
WWII World War II

Turner, Partridge, Acland, Baker, OEDS (*Oxford English Dictionary Supplement*) are among the principal collectors of slang and informal English referred to in the text; they are identified fully in the introduction. Williams is Herbert W. Williams, *A Dictionary of the Maori Language* (seventh edition, 1975, Government Printer, Wellington).

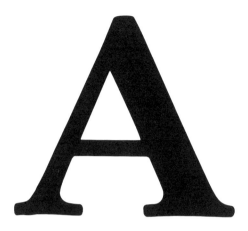

AB a woman's period, short for 'Annie Brown'; eg 'I'll have to cry off tennis today, Maureen. Old AB's visiting.' [*Shepard*]

ab-fab extreme enjoyment, short for 'absolutely fabulous'. Teen jargon 1950s and 1960s. NZA.

acid, phr. **to put the acid on** to demand something; derived from 'the acid test'; eg 'I see this new union joker's putting the acid on Lange and Douglas for more jobs.' NZA.

all around the pig's arse there is pork indicating acceptance, resignation, fatalism, in regard to a fait accompli, such as an opponent's winning snooker break.

all cock and ribs, like a musterer's dog very thin; Keri Hulme's *Te Kaihau*, 1986, uses to describe a tall, skinny man.

all hands to dance and skylark let's whoop it up, have fun; a nautical colloquialism that survived the land change. [*Jim Henderson*]

all over the place, like a madwoman's shit indicating a mess or poor organisation; eg 'That fullback's positional play is terrible. He's all over the place, like a madwoman's shit.' NZA.

angry man, the enemy soldier to Anzacs in WWII; Partridge says Australian New Guinea 1942, Jim Henderson says North Africa.

ankle-biter small child. NZA.

Anzac Australian and New Zealand Army Corps; claimed as first word formed from initials, or acronym, in modern English; WWI Australian and New Zealand soldiers. Anzac Day commemorates their disastrous, heroic landing at Gallipoli 25 April 1915.

Anzac button safety pin; nail. NZA.

Anzac hare meat loaf looking like no Anzac and no hare; for recipe refer David Burton's *Two Hundred Years of New Zealand Food and Cookery*, 1982.

Anzac shandy beer and champagne; WWI soldiers, origin of most Anzac refs, including the next entry.

Anzac wafer hard biscuit. NZA.

a over k being tipped upside down, rudely; short for 'arse over kite'.

apples in good condition, in phr. **she's apples,** indicative of apple pie order; possibly contraction of rhyming slang: 'apple and pear/fair'. NZA.
— **a bit more apple** used to indicate the need for more courage by commentator during inaugural Rugby World Cup, Wales versus Canada, 3 June 1987.

argue the toss dispute a decision; originally the toss of two-up coins. NZA.

arse into gear getting going or organised, usually as rude advice; eg 'If you don't get your arse into gear, we'll never make it on time.' NZA.

arse over tit head over heels; c.1910. NZA & Brit.

Arse-Ups, The Fourth Battalion, NZ Rifle Brigade, WWI; from shoulder flash.

arsey boo chaos, twisted, wrong; eg 'I'm going to have to say that the organisation of this reunion is all arsey boo.' [*Jim Henderson*]

arsy-tarsy all tangled up and topsy turvy; variant of 'arsy-versy'; eg 'This essay is all arsy-tarsy. You're going to have to rip it up and start again.' [*Shepard*]

artist person with notable aspect defined by preceding adjective; eg booze artist, bull artist. NZA originally, now general.

arvo afternoon (contraction of). NZA.

Auckland cove nickname for Aucklander in era of provincial governments and even more intense provincial rivalries than exist today, recorded in Thomson's *History of New Zealand*; refer Canterbury, Nelson, Otago, Taranaki and Wellington.

Aussie Australian person.

away laughing an easy start or achievement, eg 'We're away laughing on this job, mate. Should be finished by midday.' Possibly contraction of English phrase 'away you go — laughing', someone making a meal of misfortune or duty.

away with the fairies daydreaming or considered unsound in the head. NZA.

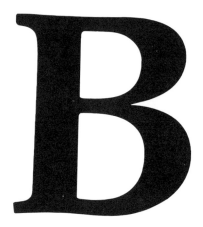

babbler cook; rhyming slang 'babbling brook/ cook', used by shearing gangs and WWI Anzacs. NZA.

bach beach or weekend cottage, c.1900. Mencken said word was still on trial in America: **baching** one or more usually male flatters or casual dwellers unused to housekeeping or living casually.

backblocks remote area; eg parts of the King Country; aka 'backwater' and 'back of beyond'; North Island word, according to Acland, replacing 'back country'; c. 1895.

bagful of busted arseholes, a an extreme state of ugliness, if preceded by 'as ugly as'; or ill health, usually owing to a hangover, if preceded by 'I feel like'. NZA.

bail up a robbery, originally by bushrangers.

— somebody blocking your progress, often requiring conversation; developed from bails, c.1851, the stalls in a milking shed to separate each cow, which developed to mean bailing up or blocking the path of a wild pig.
Both ANZ.

bait layer cook in army; originally station cook. NZA.

bang an intensive, suggesting everything, as in phr. 'the whole bang lot'; mostly NZA.

bang on dead centre; eg 'Hadlee usually bowls bang on line.'

go with a bang to go well; eg 'The party should go with a bang.'

bang goes that the end of something; eg 'A coup?! Well, bang goes that idea of yours for a holiday in Fiji.'

bang on you to nag; eg 'The cops always bang on you, eh?' [*Alison Gray*]

bangs like a dunny door, she, (in the wind) a sexually enthusiastic female. ANZ.

Barber, the the cutting Greymouth wind coming off the Mawhera River.

barbie barbecue. NZA.

barker's egg dog turd. NZA.

barker's nest pile of dog turd. [*Shepard*]

barrack support a team; Turner traces from Northern Ireland use of word as bragging, rather than Scottish use for jeering; originally a European word for soldiers' tent, 'baraque' in French, 'baracca' Italian, 'barraca' Spanish, with idea of putting a team in barracks. NZA.

barracouta oblong loaf of bread with raised crust, resembling the fish with the fearsome bite; displaced by French loaf.

base walloper Kiwi version of a base wallah, or military pen pusher; 'wallah', Hindi 'wala', connected with, was habitually added on to functions to suggest functionary in Anglo-Indian army; here refined by pun on base as bum.

bash artist brutal user of fists on others; eg 'Watch out for Morton after he's had a few drinks, becomes a real bash artist, clock you soon as look at you.'

battler conscientious worker approved of by peers; reflects antipodean recognition of life's strugglers, the word also meaning a swagman; a petty punter living on winnings; a prostitute independent of ponce or brothel; eg 'Bob has no flair, but he's a battler.' ANZ.

be in encouragement to participate, often in phr. 'be in to win'; eg 'C'mon Clive, go for the bull, be in to win.'

beaut splendid or terrific; also **beauty** and **bewdy** and even **bewdy bottler, little beaut** and **little beauty,** unto **bewdy, boy!**; eg 'Beaut racket! Where'd you get it?' Partridge says probably originally Cockney, mostly NZA.

beer goitre a large stomach or pot induced by too much of the amber fluid, aka beer; high incidence of goitre into this century here, until iodine deficiency was rectified.

beggars-on-the-coals damper or flour and water instant bread; 'beggars' euphemism for 'buggers'.

belly-buster disastrous dive where stomach hits water; aka 'bellyflop'. NZA.

berko berserk, though not really; to **go berko** is to be temporarily angry and out of control. NZA.

biddy-bid/biddy-biddy the acaena plant, Pakeha version of Maori 'piripiri'; c.1868; **biddy** to remove burrs, as characteristic of this plant; c.1880.

big-note to boast or exaggerate; eg 'Barry's big-noting again about how many he's scored over the years.' c. 1935. NZA.

big spit, the vomit, often in phr. 'to go for the big spit'. ANZ.

bikkies money; usually 'big bikkies', a lot of money. NZA.

bikie member of motorbike gang. NZA.

Bill Masseys Kiwi boots, especially military ones, named after War Minister during WWI. Obs.

billy tin pot with wire handle for boiling water over open fire, or carrying milk, the former and often the latter involved in making tea. While bully beef tins were labelled 'bouilli' and empty could be used as billies, the Aboriginal word 'billa' meaning water has a more antipodean origin than French 'bouillant', boiling; aka **billycan**. A set of billycans fitting into each other like Russian dolls are called a 'nest'. 'Billy' used Australia 1839, NZ 1853.

billycart trolley home-made from cannibalised prams and leftover bits of lumber, possibly once associated with carts pulled by billy goats.

binder meal; originally tramp slang for a satisfying meal, associated in army with constipation. NZA.

birdcage used car dealer's lot post-war; died out as dealers got rid of the chicken wire; may revive along with new security fences.

birdcage boy used car dealer.

bite your bum get lost! eg 'I'm sick of you, go bite your bum!' NZA.

bitser made from bits and pieces, such as mongrel or home-made trolley. NZA.

blackman treacle, in bread and blackman, favourite with children early this century; ref. Fred Smith, Southland, in author's *Ghost Towns of New Zealand*.

blacksmith contemptuous term for bad station cook. [*Acland*]

blades of meat feet; rhyming slang variant of English 'plates of meat'.

bless her garters kindly praise and/or thanks; variant of 'bless your little cotton socks'; the Shepards suggest the example: 'She's sewn a button on your pants, bless her garters.'

blighty blight bird, now better known as waxeye, white-eye or silver-eye.

blimey, Charlie! indicating friendly relief; obs.; derived from mostly Cockney 'blimey', abbreviation of 'Gorblimey', abbreviation of 'God blind me'. NZA.

blimin bloody or blooming; the kind of mild expletive nobody ever deleted.

blinded with science intelligence triumphing over brute strength; antipodean derivation Partridge sources from rise of scientific boxers over bruisers, notably Gentleman Jim Corbett over John L. Sullivan; Allies extended phrase in WWII to 'snowball' or bewilder somebody with a mass of scientific or technical detail.

block phr. **use your block** advice to use your common sense; **lose your block** or **do your block**, lose your temper; from C17 English word for 'head'; eg 'Docherty, if you used your block, boy, instead of losing it, you might yet make a boxer.'

blocking group rape; aka 'gang rape' or 'gangbang'; from the English word 'block', to have intercourse with a woman.

blow phr. **have a blow**, streetkid for sniffing glue. [*Alison Gray*]

blowie blowfly. NZA.

blowing/blowing off boasting or talking too much; eg 'Bill's blowing off again about his prowess with the cue.' NZA mostly.

blow that for a joke! emphatic rejection; 'blow' euphemistic curse; eg 'Me referee that lot? Blow that for a joke!'

blow up referee blowing whistle to stop play for an infringement.

bludge to cadge, scrounge or overdo acceptance of hospitality without contributing; a cardinal sin Down Under, where pioneering generosity lingers on. A **bludger** here is much milder than the English harlot's bully or bawdyhouse bouncer, or thief favouring a bludgeon.

Bludgers' Hill nickname for admin. quarters on rise of Maadi base camp near Cairo, WWII. [*Jim Henderson*]

blue red-haired man, such as 'Blue' Kennedy, secretary of the Meatworkers' Union earlier in the 1980s.
— a fight.
— a blunder.
— being drunk (as in the 'blue devils').
All NZA.

blue duck rumour, especially a baseless one or a dud; chiefly Kiwi army WWI, developed from Australian for anything not coming up to expectations.

blue rinse brigade/set middle-aged, middle-class women distinguished by blue hair and often true blue conservative point of view.

blue vinegar fit a performance manic enough to have been induced by blue vinegar, or turpentine.

bluey a summons; from the blue paper on which summonses are issued in Australia. ANZ.

blurter anus; from association with 'blurt', a sudden emission of breath. NZA.

bob hop community dance pre-WWII, entrance a 'bob' or shilling.

bobsy-die fuss or fun; common phr. 'kicking up bobsy-die'; ironic C18 English nautical almost rhyming 'bob's-a-dying/ idling' underwent sea change to NZ C19, possibly picking up 'bobbery' or shindy, from Hindi 'bapre'. Ngaio Marsh used original in *Surfeit of Lampreys*: 'If she's right . . . it plays Bobs-a-dying with the whole blooming case.' NZA.

bodgie young Australasian males in 1950s aping American and/or British fashions for duck's arse (hair swished back with excessive application of Brylcreem), poker faces, stovepipe trousers, winklepickers, given to such assertiveness the New Zealand government of the day ordered a report on this youth threat.

Origins various: English word 'bodge', to patch or mend clumsily; 'bodger', WWII slang for a worthless person; US teen slang 'bodgie' for young male jitterbug with long and curly hair and too large sports jacket; Partridge guesses distortion of 'boysies' for boys. Establishment used 'bodgie' for any young man judged a misfit or anti-social.

boil-up tea-break, mostly among thirsty trampers boiling the billy.

bomb old dilapidated car or motorbike; c.1945. NZA.

Bombay bloomers voluminous summer or sports shorts; from baggy shorts of servicemen WWII, because 'Made in Bombay'. NZA.

bong to hit, especially on the head; Aboriginal for 'dead'. ANZ.

bonzer excellent, most pleasing, attractive; possibly imported with goldrushes, from Spanish 'bonanza'; aka **bonza, boshter, bosker**. NZA. — large marble.

boohai/boo-ay/boo-eye remote area; probably corruption of Maori word Puhoi, the North Auckland Bohemian settlement so isolated early on its pioneers almost perished from hunger; phr. **up the boohai** to be lost or to have got something quite wrong, a nod perhaps at 'puhoi', Maori for dull, slow, phlegmatic; **up the boohai — shooting pukakas** (pukekos) an amusing extension of notion of being lost, possibly in the head, Sue Budd recalls. Grant Tilly recalls its completion: **up the boohai shooting pukakas with a popgun.** 'Boohai' c.1920.

boomer something first-rate or successful, such as a topnotch surfing wave, but originally a large male kangaroo; eg 'That paint job you did on the car, boomer, mate.' ANZ.

boonga offensive term for Pacific Islander, adapted from equally offensive Australian 'boong', applied to an Aboriginal.

boot in phrs. **put in the boot/put the boot in** to kick brutally, literally or metaphorically; eg 'He put the boot into Happy's chances of becoming matron by spreading the old rumour about her youthful experiment with dope.' Mostly NZA.

boot home horse racing term for kicking or urging a horse to reach the finishing line first; eg 'Jack might be losing but he's really booting his yacht home.' — any marked or forcible encouragement. Both NZA.

boots! shearing term identifying the farmer's arrival. [*Keith Slater*]

boots and all no holds barred, complete or enthusiastic commitment; eg 'What better title for big lock Andy Haden's story than *Boots 'n' All*?' NZA.

booze barn huge hotel with huge carpark, the 1970s answer for large thirsts and large profits, a social disaster on the wane.

booze artist heavy drinker of alcohol; c.1920. NZA.

boozeroo drinking bout. — pub.

borax in phr. **poke the borax** to ridicule; most popular spelling here of Aboriginal word 'borak' aka 'borac' and 'borack', perhaps because radio's Aunt Daisy was a great promoter of borax (no relation) powder as a household cleaner.

boshter first-rate, excellent; variant of 'bonzer'. NZA.

bosker first-rate, excellent; variant of 'boshter' and 'bonzer'. NZA.

bot a germ, originally in 1920s a TB patient, latterly a minor ailment, usually cold or flu; probably derived from the botfly, whose larvae feed beneath the skin, an afflicter of horses. — **to have the bot** to feel unwell or irritable. — **how're the bots biting?** a humorous greeting. — **on the bot** to cadge. NZA.

bottle drive fund raising by collecting empty bottles from residences for the miniscule deposit; now declining.

bottle-oh dealer in empty bottles, c.1900s, known from his or her cry. — a green marble. Both NZA.

bottler object of admiration or great approval; eg 'Thanks for all your help, mate. You're a bloody bottler.' NZA.

bottlie marble stopper from neck of aerated water bottle, prized by marbles buffs. NZA.

bounce the ball political test of public opinion; eg 'D'ya think Douglas is bouncing the ball again with all these rumours of a GST rise?'

bowser old-fashioned word for petrol pump, after Mr Bowser, American manufacturer of only petrol pumps available Australasia in 1930s; appropriately, 'to bowse' means to come with a rush, a drinking vessel or a drinking bout; RAF called man in charge of a towed petrol tanker a 'bowser king'.

bowyang trouser straps below knees, worn mostly by labourers. NZA.

box, phr. **the whole box and dice** everything; c.1930. ANZ.
— **in a box** confused state. [Baker]

box of birds fighting fit, NZ Services, WWII; fit and well in civilian life. Sometimes additions **and all singing, all feathers and shit**; eg 'G'day, how are ya?' 'Orrh, champion, mate. Boxa birds.'

box of fluffies/box of fluffy ducks engaging variants of preceding entry.

box on/box on regardless keep going, endure; eg 'I know we've no chance of winning, but just box on regardless.' NZA.

out of the box, (one) superb person or thing, special; eg 'That Mort's got a heart of gold. One out of the box, that joker.' c. 1930.

box seat favoured position; originally the driver's box or seat, specifically Ned 'Cabbage Tree' Devine's box seat; ref. *An Encyclopaedia of New Zealand.* So nicknamed from his headgear, Ned was a Cobb and Co. goldrush coach driver in Central Otago who won his reins by demonstrating a full coach turn on a two shillings and sixpence piece. Everybody wanted to ride his box seat. A Minister of Mines demanded it, but Ned refused him, saying the position was taken. The Minister told Ned who he was. 'Well, now,' replied Ned, 'that's a fine post. You want to see that you hang on to it.' Modern eg: 'After bowling Australia out for 125 on the first day, New Zealand look to be in the box seat in the third test at the Basin.'

box up state of confusion; eg 'It's a total box up, nobody seems to know what his position is, or what he's s'posed to do.' ANZ.

brass razoo a small amount of money; **not have a brass razoo** to have no money. Originally a gambling chip in Australasia; eg

'Sorry, chief, I'd like to help you, but I don't have a flipping brass razoo.'

bread and scrape a thrifty, minimal meal; from 1930s Depression era; eg 'Sorry kids, nothing but bread and scrape tonight.' [*Shepard*]

break it down demand to stop unacceptable behaviour; eg 'Break it down, will ya! Some of us are trying to sleep!' c. 1930s. NZA.

break up demonstrate great amusement or, contrarily, upset; eg 'He really breaks me up every time I see him.' 'Huh, that's okay for you to say. He really breaks up the poor have-nots, y'know.' NZA.

breakfast in phr. **have for breakfast** find some person or thing easy to overcome or achieve; eg 'Just let him try anything. I'll have him for breakfast.' NZA mostly.

bring in the process of introducing land to cultivation.

Brit person from **Britland**, more commonly Britain. NZA.

bronzed Anzac healthy outdoor suntanned antipodean man, such as surf lifesaver.

brown derby South Island version of a chocolate dip ice cream.

brown in phr. **do a brown** act shy or sulky or ashamed; eg 'What's wrong with Jill?' 'Nothin', Miss. She does a brown for no reason, eh.' [*Alison Gray*]

brownie originally cocoa damper or bush bread, currant loaf among shearers, treacled gingerbread cake among swaggers The Shiner knew; **brownie gorger** shearing shed hand.

Brown's cows in phr. **all over the road like Brown's cows** disorderly, disorganised or making a dreadful mess; Joy Shepard's two country aunts were crossing Christchurch's Cathedral Square with the red lights flashing, and Cousin Jack said: 'Oh gosh, Joy, look at them . . . ooh . . . all over the road like Brown's cows!'; curious recycling of the elocution improving phrase 'how now brown cow'. NZA.

bucket of bolts dilapidated car.

buckle me! exclamation of frustration; a Shepard example: 'Buckle me, look what I've done — packed the whole ruddy parcel and left out the card!' Obsolete C19 Australian 'buckle', mood; more likely euphemism.

Buckley's short for **Buckley's chance**, which is no chance; after mid-C19 Australian outlaw who was reckoned to have no chance of escape, though other explanations exist; eg 'We haven't a Buckley's of winning the cup now Honk's had to drop out of the team.' ANZ.

buggers-on-the-coals damper, with currants preferably. NZA.

buggerama exclamation of mock disgust or distress, especially in reference to oneself; eg 'I don't know how I missed that putt. It was a sitter. Buggerama!'

buggerise about aimless messing about; eg 'Stop buggerising about and get on with the game, will ya.' NZA.

buku lots of; army slang, corruption of 'beaucoup', originating in Vietnam; also US.

bull artist boaster and/or charlatan; eg 'Don't believe a word he says. That joker's a bull artist from way back.' NZA.

bulldust nonsense or reaction to the serving up of such; polite version of 'bullshit'; eg 'I'm sorry, but you're just talking absolute bulldust.'

bullocky bullock driver and the colourful language he was known for from earliest times, notably the drunken, foul-mouthed Sam of whom Edward Jerningham Wakefield writes in *Adventure in New Zealand* calling his bullocks by the names of the magistrates who fined him for bad language and for flogging his beasts.
— **to bullock** is still regarded as acting belligerently, and rugby forwards, in commentators' parlance, **bullock over** for tries.
— **bullocky's joy** treacle or golden syrup. All NZA.

bullsh nonsense; short for 'bullshit'. NZA.

bullswool nonsense, or exclamation at serving up of; tenuous link to tenuous fibre of stringy-bark gum tree; c.1920. ANZ.

bully first rate; Meade's *New Zealand*, 1870, refers to a 'bully blaze' while English used the word only to refer to people. NZA and US.

bum bandit male homosexual.

bum man heterosexual male with professed liking for female buttocks, in phr. 'I'm a bum man myself'.

bum nuts eggs. [*Shepard*]

bun phr. **do your bun** lose your temper; eg 'Hey, no need to do your bun, Milt. You'll get your money.'

bun hat bowler hat.

bung ruined or bankrupt, often in phr. **to go bung**; Aboriginal word for 'dead'; eg 'After the stockmarket crash, his business went bung.' ANZ.

bung it on skite, exaggerate, behave temperamentally; common among antipodean shearers.

bunking wagging school.

burk to avoid work, c.1880-1920; G.B. Lancaster in *Sons o' Men*: 'I'll exchange . . . but I won't burk, see?'

burn drive a vehicle fast, phr. **go for a burn**, originally a bikie's **burn-up**; a **burn off** to drive so fast you leave the competition behind; eg 'Let's go for a burn, eh?' 'Dunno, don't think we could burn off old Scotty, now he's got that rebore.' NZA.

bush forest.
— **go bush** leave the city for the simple wild life; suddenly do so, unexpectedly, to dismay of those you know; eg 'Since the crash nobody's seen hair nor hide of Rex. He's gone bush.'
— **beat about the bush** prevaricate; eg 'Don't beat about the bush — either you know the answer or you don't.'
All NZA except for 'bush' itself, which in Australia can be open countryside.

bushed exhausted; lost; eg 'Can we take a breather? I'm bushed.' NZA.

bushwhacked exhausted; eg 'No more for me. I'm utterly bushwhacked.' NZA.

bushman's breakfast a yawn, a stretch, a piss and a look round. ANZ.

bushman's dinner mutton, damper and tea.

bush baptist religious fundamentalist or religious poseur; first used in Boer War. NZA.

bush carpenter self-taught or rough and ready carpenter. NZA.

bush lawyer unqualified practitioner of the law or argumentative legalistic type; NZA.
— native thorny vine; c.1853.

bush mechanic rough and ready, unqualified mechanic.

bust it! dash it!; eg 'I almost had it that time. Oh bust it!' NZ and Brit., early C20.

busy as a one-armed paperhanger bustling busy; c. 1939, also Canadian.

butchers to be angry, often **go butchers**; short for 'butcher's hook', rhyming slang for 'go crook at' — English rhyming version a 'look'; eg 'That teacher's always going butchers.' NZA.

buttendski bum; Jim Henderson sources to polite Kaipara teenagers 1920s.

buttinski to butt in or interrupt, usually not welcomed; Kiwi soldiers 1915, a mock coinage; subsequently travelled to Australia, and heard by author in American TV series *MASH*.

buttonhole to crutch sheep's sensitive areas; from 'buttonhole' as vagina or penis. [*Shepard*]

by the limping cricket agreeable or exasperated oath akin to 'by thunder' or 'by crikey', used Kaipara area 1920s; eg 'By the limping cricket, you're a useless darned goory.' [*Jean and Jim Henderson*]

by the thundering sardine agreeable or mock horror oath of the 'by crikey' variety; eg 'By the thundering sardine, that's a crop and a half of spuds you've got this year.' [*Jean Henderson*]

BYO acronym for bring your own, usually meaning the wine you take to an unlicensed restaurant. NZA.

cabbaging smoking dope leaves, inferior product. [*Alison Gray*]

cactus phr. **in the cactus** in difficulties; eg 'The recent defections have put the club in the cactus.' Derived from appreciation of American desert growth. NZA.

Canterbury pilgrim mid-C19 nickname for person from Canterbury.

Captain Cooker wild pig the good captain introduced; also a **cooker**, described by Edward Jerningham Wakefield as 'a gaunt, ill-shaped or sorry looking pig'.

cark collapse or die, of person or machine, in phr. **cark it** to die, **cark out** to collapse into a drunken stupor; possibly derived from slaughtered carcass of an animal; eg 'When the scrum collapsed on Rippin, I thought he was goin' to cark.' NZA.

carn! shortened form of the encouragement 'come on!' used frequently by antipodean sporting spectators; eg 'Hey, youse jokers, we can make the ferry if we step on it. Carn, will ya.'

carnie sexually desirable and probably available female under the lawful age of 16 for sexual intercourse, short for 'carnal knowledge'; aka 'jailbait', because of jail sentence for male convicted of carnal knowledge. NZA.

carry Matilda to carry one's swag or 'matilda'; NZ variant of Australian 'waltz Matilda'.

cat's bar ladies' bar or lounge bar of hotel where women permitted, as opposed to all-male traditional public bar; eg Gordon Slatter's *A Gun in My Hand*: 'He's a randy old coot always hanging around the cat's bar.'

cattle dog Protestant term of abuse for a Catholic.

caught short to be surprised without supplies of money, hospitality, etc; eg 'Look, lass, you've caught me short. Can you come back a bit later, when the wife's home? She'll buy your Girl Guide biscuits. She thinks they're grouse.' — a sudden need to urinate or defecate, or menstruate with no tampons available. NZA.

cave in to defecate; Tom Scott sources to Feilding freezing works.

chair phr. **in the chair** your turn to buy the group's drinks; eg 'Ah, Morrie, you're in the chair, boy. C'mon, I'm thirsty.' NZA.

charge like a wounded bull excessive prices; pun on charge; eg 'Sure, nice gear, but she charges like a wounded bull for it.'

cheap charlie tightwad; army slang borrowed from Saigon bar girls. Also US.

cheeri! cheerio, c.1930.

cheerio cocktail sausage.

cheese phr. **cut the cheese** to fart; eg 'Okay, who cut the cheese?' A cheeser was C18 English for a strong-smelling fart.

chelsea sugar; from the name of the sugar works.

cherry new ball in cricket, phr. **taking the cherry**, c.1950. ANZ.

chew a kumara topdressing plane crash; evolved to **suck a kumara**, when something seizes, such as a car engine; eg 'Is that South End Motors? Yeh, Dave here. The old Rover's sucked the kumara again.'

chews sweets or lollies, originally chewing gum handed out by Americans here during WWII.

chiack mock, tease, disparage, usually by sporting spectators, used

26

by commentator in 1987
World Rugby Cup;
originally English
costermonger greeting
'chiike' (or 'chy-ack',
'chiack' and 'chihike'); here
c.1890. NZA.

chillybin polystyrene
picnic hamper for keeping
food and particularly drink
cool. NZA.

chinaman unshorn lock on
the sheep's rump, which
Straight Furrow magazine,
21 February 1968,
explained was 'like the
pigtail of Orientals'.

chip at/chip away at
undermine someone with
unpleasant criticism;
originally shearing term
for finding fault with work
of a shearer; eg 'If you
keep on chipping away at
him about his maths, he's
going to fail everything.
You know the boy's not
very confident.' NZA.

chippie a potato chip.

chockie chocolate. NZA.

choke a darkie to
defecate. ANZ.

choke it cancel or stop
something; eg 'Shall I
choke the telly? There's
nothing worth watching
tonight.' [*Shepard*]

chook domestic fowl.
— woman.
— silly person.
All NZA.
— Kiwi army signal corps,
from alleged habit of
running around with their
heads cut off; hence phr.
**run around like a headless
chook/like a chook with
its head cut off**
compounding the panic.

chookie girlfriend or
young woman.

chook's bum the mouth.
ANZ.

choom British person;
'chum' pronounced in
Northern English accent.
NZA.

chop share or cut; phr. **in
for one's chop** selfishly
interested in getting one's
share and perhaps more;
from the best cut of sheep
or beef carcass; eg 'Any
hint of extra profits and
Nat's in for his chop, no
worries.' C. 1920,
Australia c.1940.
— **not much chop** of little
value; from Anglo-Indian
'first chop', first rate, from
Hindi 'chhap', a print, seal
or brand; eg 'All the fuss
about this new
supermarket. Prices are no
different. I don't think it's
much chop myself.' NZA.

chow offensive term for Chinese from mid-C19. NZA.

Chrissie Christmas, usually in 'Chrissie presents'. NZA.

Christchurch!/by Christchurch!/by Christchurch, hooya? euphemistic extension of exclamation 'by Christ!', the 'hooya' short for 'who are you?' a juvenile addition; Partridge suggests a 'Maorified' shape of 'by crikey, who are you?'

chuck to vomit; often 'have a chuck'.
— **chuck a mental** behave in a startling fashion or lose one's temper.
— **chuck in/chuck it in** to resign or leave a job.
— **chuck it in** to give up; eg 'Most of us miss a wave we might throw a bit of a wobbly, but Parrot chucks a mental. I reckon he ought to chuck in surfing or making surfboards, or both.' All NZA.

chuddy or **chutty** chewing gum. NZA.

chuff buttocks; from Durham dialect word used in England to mean a lumbar thrust to stimulate male member during coition, in America to mean pubic hair; on 30 July 1967 Prime Minister Keith Holyoake was reported by the Christchurch *Star* as saying somebody was 'sitting on his chuff', meaning he was sitting back and doing nothing, ie he was lazy.

chug to drink alcohol; **chugalug** act of drinking, usually a beer, in one gulp, or a drinking bout; eg 'Fancy a few chugs after work, Nobby?' ANZ.

chunder vomit; rhyming slang 'Chunder Loo/spew' early this century, from advertisements featuring a character Chunder Loo promoting Cobra boot polish in *The Bulletin* magazine from 8 April 1909; nautical shout 'watch under!' and English dialect 'chounter', or 'chunter' or 'chunder', to grumble, are less likely origins. ANZ.

clayie clay marble.

clever gear smart clothes; sometimes slightly derisive observation; eg 'I see you've got the clever gear on tonight. Got a new sheila lined up, have ya, Tonksy?' — new machinery; eg 'That clever gear should do wonders for the bakery.'

clobbering machine, the the way in which the system is alleged to command conformity by squashing people who stand out, cutting tall poppies down to everybody's size, the tyranny of the mediocre, the dark side of egalitarianism — or sour grapes from those frustrated by conformity or slowed down by rules and regulations. Somewhat dated by Rogernomics.

clucky showing signs of wanting children, being pregnant, or being fussy about children, akin to the clucking of a broody hen; eg 'Win's been quite clucky of late. You haven't duffed her, have you, Brian?' NZA.

Coaster person from the West Coast of the South Island.

coat-hanger stiff, one-armed neck tackle in rugby, dangerous and illegal.

cobber mate, friend, from Yiddish 'chaber', a comrade. NZA.

cobber up with make friends with; eg 'I cobbered up with Barry over the duck-shooting season, but I haven't seen him since.'

cockabully cute Pakeha version of Maori 'kokopu', or grayling, a small freshwater fish; c.1882.

cocky farmer, usually in a small way; contraction of 'cockatoo', the Australian crested parrot, whom farmers were presumed to resemble in trying to scratch a living off a small piece of land; Turner notes use by convicts pre-1852 of a petty criminal. ANZ.

cocky's joy treacle or golden syrup, a favoured spead on bread in less affluent days in poorer and usually rural parts. ANZ.

cocky's string fencing wire, called 'cocky's friend' in Australia. [Turner]

coconut insulting nickname for a Pacific Islander.

colonial goose boned and stuffed leg of mutton bearing some resemblance to a goose; once regarded as a national dish both sides of the Tasman. David Burton provides a dinkum recipe in his *Two Hundred Years of New Zealand Food and Cookery.*

come to light with to supply; eg 'She came to light with a plate of sausage rolls just when we were about to ring out for a pizza.' NZA.

come up against to meet difficulties; eg 'You can come up against some pretty stiff opposition in social grade rugby, but not often.' NZA.

Commo a Communist. NZA.

compo compensation for lost wages from work-related injury, formalised as Accident Compensation.
— **on compo** in receipt of such.
— **compo king** malingerer or self-mutilator, with the aim of getting compo.
All NZA.

Constantinople! euphemism for 'Christ almighty!'

cooee Aboriginal call adapted by Australasian attention-seekers and housewives.
— **within cooee** able to be hailed.
— **not within cooee** far from achieving a goal.
All ANZ.

Cook's Tourists Second Echelon, 2NZEF, WWII, because they went to Britain. [*Jim Henderson*]

cootie head louse, from Maori and Polynesian 'kutu', louse, and not unlike the Hindi word 'khuthi', a scab, used in army slang as 'cootie' to refer to body louse, and the Malayan 'cootie', a dog tick.

coral stomper Pacific Islander; mildly offensive.

cossie a swimming costume. NZA.

cot case lunatic or very drunk, fit only for a cot or baby's enclosed bed. NZA.

couldn't fuck a frog trotting said of a person less than ept. [*Jim Henderson*]

couldn't see the road to the dunny if it had red flags on it said of somebody slow-witted or blind drunk.

couldn't sell a statue to a pigeon derisive remark about an ineffectual person.

cow unpleasant, mean, ill-tempered person or unco-operative thing, such as 'a cow of a lawnmower'. NZA.

cowbang to run a dairy farm. NZA. Also **cowspank**.

cowbanger dairy farmer. NZA.

cow cocky dairy farmer. NZA.

cowspanker dairy farmer. NZA.

cowsh nonsense, short for 'cowshit'. NZA.

cow's kipper cow dung. 'Look out there,' her mother would warn young Joy Shepard, 'you'll go for a skate on a cow's kipper.'

coz greeting of friend, short for cousin; a Kiwi revival of archaic greeting used by likes of Romeo and Benvolio in Shakespeare's *Romeo and Juliet*.

crack to hit, as in Frank S. Anthony's *Me and Gus*; something achieved, as in **crack a fat**, a male erection and/or ejaculation; **crack a greenie**, riding a wave or opening a bottle of beer. NZA.

cracker excellent, highly approved; from a small cord at the end of stockwhip
— **can he crack his whip?** is he a good drinking man?
— **not to have a cracker** without funds; c. 1920.
— **not worth a cracker** of virtually no value; c.1920. All NZA.

cracker cartridge; c.1900.

crash hot! excellent. NZA.

cray 100 dollar bill; from its colour red, same as a crayfish; eg Bold poker player to the table: 'His cray and up two.'

crayfish a crawler or contemptible schemer; from army WWI; eg 'That ruddy Miller's the crayfish round here. Next time one of us is done, he cops a bunch of fives.'

cream your jeans to act excessively excited, even unto the actual expression of sperm, though usually not; eg 'The first time he sat in his new Jag he almost creamed his jeans.' ANZ.

crib weekend or beach cottage in South Island; c.1862.
— cut lunch on the West Coast of South Island, appearing as such in coalminer awards, moving with dam workers into Central Otago. In C19 England a 'crib' was lodgings or a public house, mentioned in Dickens' *Oliver Twist*.

cronk ill; originally among shearers; since 1880s of a horse made to appear ill to cheat its backers; from German 'krank', ill. NZA.

crook sick, dishonest, unhealthy, unpleasant people, and things out of order. Endless antipodean permutations, of which some are:
— **crook deal** fate not being nice to you.
— **crook do** rotten party.
— **crook job** rotten job.
— **crook run** unlucky period.
— **crook steer** misleading information.
— **crook trot** unlucky period.
Overheard in North Auckland pub: 'Gee, this beer's crook.' 'Yeah, I'll be glad when I've had enough.' [*Turner*]

— **go crook at** be angry with; **put someone crook** give bad advice.
— **in crook with** in trouble with somebody, or out of favour.

cross-eyed spieler a glib or crafty fellow, encountered in Frank S. Anthony's *Me and Gus*, could be originally from Australia, c.1905; from Yiddish 'spiel', to play, used generally in English to mean sales patter or swindling, usually at cards.

cuff phr. **on the cuff** excessive or unfair or inappropriate; perhaps rhyming collocation 'a bit rough', suggests OEDS; eg 'Steady on, old boy, that language is a bit on the cuff.' Late C19. NZA.

cunning as a Maori dog very cunning or sly; Gordon Slatter, *A Gun in My Hand*.

cupful of cold sick, a a shock, often used to describe how something is received or how one feels or how little something is valued in the phrase 'not worth a cupful of cold sick', a variation of the Australian colloquialism 'not worth a cupful of cold water'.

cuppa cup of tea; c.1905. NZA.

curly a difficult situation, derived possibly from googly ball in cricket; eg 'That second question on the exam paper's a curly one.' Mostly ANZ since 1950.

Currie boy bikie frequenting Currie's milkbar, Queen Street, Auckland, in the 1950s.

curry-muncher Indian; offensive. Mostly ANZ.

cut share; late C19; **in for one's cut** expecting one's share of profit; eg 'Hey, I contributed to that winning ticket. Where's my cut?'

cut to finish or finished; eg 'Let's cut all the beer.' 'Too late. It's all cut.'

cuts corporal punishment in antipodean schools; eg 'It wasn't fair the whole class getting the cuts, old Jolly knew which ones were the culprits.'

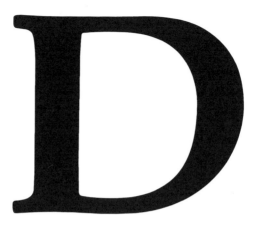

dag, daggy amusing person or thing, memorably in Fred Dagg, rural comic creation of urban Kiwi John Clarke in 1970s, dressed in black woollen farmer's singlet, muddy shorts and gumboots, an apparently dim but actually canny cocky; exported to Australia, whence word originated c.1890, says Partridge, who thinks it probably comes from 'dagen', or 'degen', German for sword, 'dagen' in English meaning an artful criminal or criminal type. Common uses indicating amusement are:
— **what a dag** of a person or thing.
— **a bit of a dag** of a person.

— 'dag' an excrement-coated wool clot around sheep's anus, is the origin of another popular antipodean phr. **rattle your dags!** hurry up!

Dallie a Dalmatian New Zealander whose forebears came in the 1890s, before there was a Yugoslavia back home, to dig gum in Northland, and then founded our wine industry.

Dallie plonk the often rough and usually red wine sold here mid-century, when most Kiwis were beer drinkers, before the Dalmatians got their wine act together and Kiwis started drinking the grape, c.1960s.

damper bush bread of flour and water cooked on coals, usually unleavened, though sometimes leavened by soaking water in ashes overnight, or by using baking powder, baking soda, fruit salts or bore water, sometimes with addition of sugar, fat, currants or cocoa, the cocoa damper being called 'brownie'; c.1825. ANZ.

date anus; 'get off your date' was common army advice WWII. NZA.

daylight robbery shameless overcharging; eg 'Electricity charges these days are daylight robbery.' Mostly NZA.

dead phr. **enough/fit to wake the dead** very loud; eg 'Shut up, Sean, that screaming is fit to wake the dead.' NZA.

dead as a moa very dead; our variant of dodo; also **dead as a rat**.

deadman buried anchor adapted to support fenceposts.

dead ring exact likeness; eg David Ballantyne, *The Cunninghams*, 1948, writing of the sons: 'They were the dead ring of Gil.' NZA. Aka 'dead ringer', also US.

Debt Dodgers and Wife Beaters First Echelon, 2NZEF, WWII, used derisively even by the volunteers themselves; perhaps originating fro.n media comment at the time, Jim Henderson speculates.

Deep Thinkers Fifth Reinforcements, 2NZEF, WWII, from one saying: 'I did some deep thinking before deciding to join up.' [*Jim Henderson*]

delec desirable, of person or thing, short for delectable; 1960s teen jargon; eg 'Isn't Troy Donahue just delec!'

delish short for delicious, another teen fave-rave; eg 'Troy Donahue? He's just delish!'

Diamond Dinks Second Battalion, NZ Rifle Brigade, WWI, from shoulder flash.

diarrhoea bags knickerbockers; recalled in NZ Oral History Unit Martinborough study.

dibs marbles; originally dibstones, a children's game with small stones or sheep's knucklebones. NZA.

dicken disgust or disbelief or surprised belief, in form of an interjection, largely replaced by 'really!' or 'really?'; an antipodean contraction of 'the dickens' or 'what the dickens!', being a euphemism for the devil.
— **dicken on that!** go easy, will you!; eg 'You want me to help you lift that dirty big post? Dicken on that, mate.'

dickey stupid; eg 'Well, I don't think Billy T's dickey at all, I think he's neat.' [*Alison Gray*]

dickhead silly person: **dickheaded** stupid, from military slang 'dick', penis; eg 'Morgan's dropped the ball again. What a dickhead!' Both NZA.

didn't have sixpence to jingle on a tombstone imperial assessment of a poor person, recorded by Stevan Eldred-Grigg in *Oracles and Miracles*, 1987, of pre-WWII NZ.

digger Anzac soldier; originally a goldminer or digger; used in a matey greeting. NZA.

dill, dillbrain silly or incompetent person, possibly from daffodil, where 'daffy' means daft; eg 'Wear ear-muffs with that weedeater, dillbrain.' NZA.

ding a dent, usually in a car, of a minor nature; also the minor accident itself; probably from archaic English word meaning 'to strike'; eg 'Don't get your knickers in a twist, Mum, it's only a ding in your new Honda.' NZA.

dingbat odd or silly person; plural form means madness, either of rage or delirium tremens; singular was an Anzac officer's servant in WWI, said to be a merger of dingo and batman. ANZ.

dinkum genuine or fair, often expressed as **fair dinkum, dinky-di** and **dinkum oil** (the truth), and as **dinkum Kiwi**; popularised in Australasia from Lincolnshire dialect word 'dinkum', an equitable share of work, and 'fair dinkum', fair play, with Gloucestershire and Derbyshire dialects also regarding dinkum as working hard; eg 'Some of those words you've collected are the dinkum Kiwi oil all right.'

dinky/dinky-di true; 'Hadlee better than Lillee? Dinky-di, mate.' ANZ.

dinnyhayser anything first-rate; eg 'So that's your new yacht. She's a dinnyhayser, boy.' From Australian boxer Dinny Hayes. [*Shepard*] ANZ.

dip one's lid honour or congratulate, originally by raising one's hat. NZA.

dip out fail; eg 'You'll need a good line with her, Clem. Better men than you have dipped out there.' NZA.

dip south put hand in pocket for money, especially if running out of it; NZA variant of English 'put down south'.

dipper, phr. **in your dipper!** expression of defiance between world wars; possibly ref. to sheep dip.

do, do in to spend all one's money, often recklessly; eg 'Promise you'll come straight home, Harold. You know if you go to the TAB you'll do in your entire pay packet.'
— to defeat; eg 'With Kirwan playing they'll do your team.'
Both NZA.

do a get hasty retreat; eg 'C'mon, youse jokers, let's do a get before old Musty catches us.' c. 1900. NZA.

do over to beat up; the Maungatapu murderers spoke of 'doing over' their victims in 1866.
— redecorate; eg 'What do you say we do over the bathroom next year, Billy?' Both NZA.

dob to kick.
— **dob in** to betray; to contribute funds; to put someone in trouble, perhaps oneself; eg 'Watch your step with him, he'll dob you in for the hell of it.'
— **dob on** to betray, eg 'If you tell the whole world you haven't paid tax for 10 years, somebody's going to dob on you.'
— **dob over** kick a goal in rugby, often by drop kick; from English dialect word 'dob', to throw down heavily.
All NZA.

dogbox cramped quarters, originally the guard's van cage; **in the dog box** out of favour, in disgrace; eg 'I see Jim's staying at the pub again. In the dogbox with his missus, eh?'

doglegged shape of a crooked fence; from the proverbially crooked nature of a dog's hind leg, now more familiar in the dogleg approach to some golf holes. NZA.

dog trials test of dog skill in controlling sheep, described famously by John Gordon in annual TV series.

dog tucker mutton scraps or food humans would not fancy, served up to working dogs. Sometimes used to describe a poor looking sheep or other beast, 'fit only for dog tucker'. NZA.

dommyknocker a stick to beat other kids with, aka **bommyknocker**; origins unknown, though a 'dommie' was a nickname for a Norton 'Dominator' motorbike and thus for any motorcyclist, while 'bommie' is a bombora or submerged reef beyond beach breakers, of interest only to Australian surfers, and their guests.

dong to strike or punch, perhaps from the sound of the word; eg 'If you don't piss off quick smart, I'll dong you one.' NZA.

donger penis, by association with preceding entry. NZA.

don't be anky-fooken thanks but no thanks, a retort rejecting some suggestion that does not appeal as your cup of tea, or seems a bit over the fence. [Shepard]

doodackie thingummybob, or humorous word for something you have no name for; a local variation of doodad, doodah, dooflickey, etc.

dook to duck, obsolete form, used by Kiwi kids in **dooking for apples**, ducking head beneath the surface of the water to recover floating apples using only teeth; recorded by Brian Sutton-Smith in his collection of children's games.

doolan Roman Catholic, usually expected to be Irish; presumably from Doolan being a common Irish name here last century.

dork stupid person, now also so used in England, where it had once meant the lower classes, by association with literal meaning of a doorstep;

here derived from meaning a penis. Also US.

doub/dub/dubb short for 'doubling', in context of giving someone a lift on your bike; Australians prefer 'double-bank' or 'double-dink'.

doughboy dumpling of flour, sugar and suet, a favourite when out mustering; in America it is flour and rice-based. NZA.

down, in phr. **have a down on** a grudge, hostile or at least poor opinion of someone; in 1862 Charles Thatcher said he had 'no down on Travers'. NZA.

down the road where sacked people are sent.

down trou male (usually) party trick of standing on the table and dropping trousers, shared with certain Brits, as author witnessed when several All Blacks and Lions rugby players downtrou-ed in a Wellington restaurant in 1983.

Down Under New Zealand and Australia, as perceived from the Northern Hemisphere

dozo fool, variant of dozy.

drac(k) awful or ugly, as in Dracula. NZA.

dragging the chain holding up a group's activities, such as a drinking school; originally the slowest shearer in the shed; eg 'Larry's dragging the chain again on keeping his berm mowed.' NZA.

drive the pigs home to snore; in England the phrase is: 'drive the pigs to market'.

driver is safer when the road is dry, The/And the road is safer when the driver is dry homily against drinking and driving. [Shepard]

drongo slow-witted person; probably early 1920s Australian racehorse of that name which never won, the horse most likely getting its name from the bird; eg 'Gabe's a complete drongo when it comes to driving in rush-hour traffic, though otherwise he's competent enough.' NZA.

drop to hit somebody with the intention of flattening them; eg 'One more crack out of you and I'll drop ya.'

drop hundreds and thousands lose weight, especially around the waist; from dropping the coloured cake decorations '100s and 1000s' and picking them up one at a time, thus losing weight around the waist. [*Shepard*]

drop in it put someone in trouble; eg 'You really dropped me in it with the wife telling her I was the one wanting another round.'

drop one's bundle to despair or give birth; eg 'Sam's dropped his bundle ever since that triple bogey on the 18th when he was four clear.'

drop one's gear to get undressed; eg 'Drop your gear and let's see what you're made of.'

drop one's load a male ejaculation; eg 'Corky's your one-night stand type — drops his load and off, never seen again.'

drop off to drive somebody where they want to go, or to stop pressuring somebody; eg 'I'll drop you off at the next layby' or 'There's been a drop off in Spassky's endgame of late,

don't you think?' All 'drop' phrases NZA.

dropper fence batten. NZA.

drummer swagman or tramp. NZA.

dry as a wooden god very dry or thirsty; popular NZ Navy WWII.

dry balls bastard cricket c/p for a bowler who gives nothing away.

dub in to contribute to a kitty or collection; eg 'Are you dubbing in for her going away present?' Local variant of 'dub up', pay up, mid-C19 English slang.

duckshove to cheat or pass responsibility on to someone else, perceived as a typical bureaucratic trick; eg 'The public is always complaining of duckshoving in that department.' Originally cabbies jumping the queue in mid-C19 Melbourne cab ranks. ANZ.

duck's breakfast or **dinner** a drink of water to WWI soldiers.

ducks on the pond warning of a woman in a male environment; shearing term. [*Keith Slater*]

duff to make pregnant, developed from British phrase 'up the duff', to be pregnant; eg 'You know why he married her, don't you? Because he duffed her, of course.' NZA.

dumb-bum dolt; eg 'C'mon, dumb-bum, concentrate and you might manage to hit the ball.'

dummy punishment cell in prison.
— practice of taking up land allegedly for yourself, but on behalf of another, usually a friend or relative acting for a squatter. NZA.

dump one's load male ejaculation (vomit in America); eg 'Cec dumped his load and was snoring within minutes.' NZA.

dunga, dunger trouble, in phr. **in the dunga**; perhaps extension of word 'dung'.
— dilapidated object, such as house, car or contraption, from engine going 'dunga, dunga, dunga', the word serving to indicate the object is useless.
— penis, perhaps combining 'donger' and 'punga', the tree fern with the suggestive penis shape.

dungpuncher active male homosexual. NZA.

dunny toilet, a shortened form of English word 'dunnyken', a night cart, from 'danna', shit. Among many calls upon the word in c/ps:
— **swings like a dunny door** cricket term for a free-swinging and perhaps inept batsman. ANZ. Refer 'bangs like a dunny door'.

durry cigarette, usually roll-your-own, the makings often called **durries**, perhaps associated with Bill Durham brand tobacco, though Partridge ponders possible link with 'duria', fire; eg 'Fling us your durries, will ya, mate. I'm dying for a smoke.' c. 1910. NZA.

41

e hoa! greeting or hailing or expression of amazement, colloquialism from Maori 'friend'.

earbash to talk, perhaps to harangue; eg 'Give him half a chance and he'll earbash you all night.' NZA.

early shower what you can take after the ref has ordered you off the field of play for illegal activity.

earwag to harangue, but mildly, or to gush gossip; eg 'While the girls are earwagging, fancy a game, old boy?'

easies women's elasticised foundation garment, called 'step-ins' in Australia.

eat toot accepting local conditions; a reference to 'tutu', the poisonous plant, in the saying of new immigrants last century, meaning they must settle for the cold hard facts of pioneer life. Obs.

eggs are cooked, one's something undesirable and probably inevitable which somebody has suffered; eg 'After droughts two years running, his eggs were well and truly cooked.' c. 1910.

el fabuloso! exclamation of approval among 1960s DJs and some of their listeners; an early example of Tex-Mex influence.

empty sack can't stand, An/and a full sack can't bend farmer's homily urging casual labourers to work good and hard at harvest time. [*Shepard*]

En Zed phonetically New Zealand, its inhabitants **En Zedders**.

extra enhancing intensive which can reverse the meaning of the parent word, as in the first of the two common uses of it following:
— **extra curly** first rate; eg 'That last four Martin Crowe belted was extra curly'; c.1935.

— **extra grouse** exceptionally attractive; eg 'The spread put on by Ken's Mum after the game was extra grouse.' Often applied to a desired woman; possibly derived from the gamebird 'grouse'.

eyes out as fast as possible; a variation of the Australian convict era phrase 'to go eyes out', to work very hard; eg 'Okay, lads, eyes out and we'll be through this by three.' ANZ.

fair buck appeal for fairness or reasonable treatment; eg 'Fair buck, you guys, I've only been batting a few minutes.'

fair crack (of the whip) ditto above. NZA.

fair cow another variation on the egalitarian thirst for reasonable treatment; eg 'Fair cow, sir, I've swabbed down the boats twice and Jimmy hasn't even done it once.'

fair do yet another appeal, sometimes **fair dos**; eg 'Oh, fair dos, don't I get a turn?'

fair go the most popular appeal of all; originally the call in two-up game to indicate everything was in order, the betting was closed and the spinner would toss the coins. NZA.

fair shake (of the dice)/ fair suck of the sav/ saveloy/sauce stick/fair whack are some more appeals for fairness. NZA.

fan-bloody-tastic! jocularly wonderful!; a popular use of 'bloody' as an infix, common elsewhere in, for example, 'abso-bloody-lutely'; eg 'Bruce batted through the innings, a whole day and a half out there in 40 plus. Fan-bloody-tastic, mate! No other word for it.'

fantidilyastic 1960s teen slanguage straining to get beyond fantabulous; eg 'This new lime milkshake is . . . ooohhh . . . just fantidilyastic!'

fat show little or no chance, or 'fat chance' (used in America too); eg 'Fat show we've got of making the finals.'

fend off to take or steal; c.1932.

Fernleaf New Zealander, from the badge worn by WWI soldiers; replaced by 'Kiwi'.

finickity fussy; combining finicky and pernickety; eg 'That kid's so finickity about her food, I'm surprised she doesn't look half starved.' ANZ.

firing a warmer into the bank the first beer; from army slang for first round fired to get the range.

fish hooks difficulties; eg 'Any fish hooks in the report?'

fit as a buck rat strong, healthy and athletic. [*Slatter*]

fitter and turner army cook, who fits food into pots and turns it.

fix bayonets methylated spirits; variant of military term for Bermuda rum, with ref. its sting; WWII army. [*Jim Henderson*]

flags, phr. **have the flags out** menstrual period; popularised by Barry Humphries' appalling Ocker persona Bazza McKenzie bewailing this barrier to his chances of scoring. ANZ.

flakers drooping drunk and on the way out; eg 'For Pete's sake don't buy Beech another round. Can't you see he's flakers?' NZA.

flap off go away; eg 'Why don't you flap off, eh?' [*Jim Henderson*]

flat stick as fast as the vehicle will travel; eg 'He was going flat stick, but the cop was gaining on him.'

flat tack as fast as you can get yourself or your vehicle to go; eg 'She took the corner flat tack and somehow got round it on two screeching, smoking tyres.'

flattie a punctured tyre; eg 'She's given the old dunga too hard a time on the corners, she got a flattie on the back left and flapped to a stop.'

flaxie flax worker, as obsolete as the industry making rope from flax.

flea taxi a sheepdog pup.

flea track hair parting; eg 'Make a nice straight flea track now.' [*Shepard*]

fleeco/fleecy shearing hand who picks up the shorn fleeces; late C19. ANZ.

floater a pie floating in gravy served up traditionally by piecarts and cafeterias along with peas and lumpy mashed potato. NZA.
— a turd that will not flush away.

float up casual approach, unexpected arrival or departure; ref. Gordon Slatter's *A Gun in My Hand*. NZA.

flog off to depart; eg Gordon Slatter's *A Gun in My Hand*: 'Was gonna give him a buncha five [fist] but I flogged off instead.'

fly cemetery dried fruit mix in pastry sandwich, usually currants, sometimes called a **squashed fly cemetery** if sultanas; in English boarding schools a currant pudding.

fob Samoan; street talk.

fong methylated spirits. [*Jim Henderson*]

fonged drunk.

fonged up drunk, cluttered, messed up, bewildered, stymied; combining fog and pong; eg 'He's all fonged up about whether or not she likes him.'

frog's eyes boiled tapioca or sago, as usually inflicted on those in institutions; variant of Australian 'frog's eggs', English 'frogspawn'.

frogskin French letter or contraceptive sheath. NZA.

froudacious inaccurate; from historian Froude's comments on Australia and New Zealand, c.1880, coined from 'Froude' and 'audacious'; ref. Farmer and Henley's *Slang and its Analogues*. Obs.

frozen nothing happening; eg 'Manners Mall's frozen these days, eh? Too many cops.' [*Alison Gray*]

fuck-knuckle idiot, often amiably applied; eg 'G'day, fuck-knuckle. How's it goin'? NZA.

fuckwit a fool.
— **fuckwitted** very foolish; eg 'That's the most fuckwitted idea I've ever heard.'
Both NZA.

full as a boot/bull/ Catholic school/goog (egg) very drunk. NZA.

full tit maximum effort, usually from a car; eg 'I gave her full tit, man, and we were still only doin' 70.' NZA.

full up exasperated, weary, disgusted; eg 'I'm full up with this shower, Netty. Let's split.' NZA.

Fuller's Earth New Zealand; Fuller Brothers theatres and cinemas spanned the land 1910-30. — **a Fuller's** any vaudeville show.

funny insolent; eg 'Are you trying to be funny?'; phr. **It's not funny** hey, listen, I'm serious. NZA.

funny (or silly) as a piece of string very funny; often used ironically; eg. 'That toddler with her eyebrow-raising is as funny as a piece of string.'

futuparu cod-Maori for rugby, Maori being 'hutuporo' for football.

GAFU God Almighty fuck-up; the WWII NZ Second Expeditionary Force variation of the RAF's SNAFU (Situation Normal All Fucked Up), usually a reference to decisions that landed fighting men in impossible situations. [*Jim Henderson*]

gangway for a naval officer make way there, get out of the way; Partridge says common among WWI Kiwi soldiers.

gate mouth; WWI soldiers; eg 'Shut your gate, mate, or I'll shut it for you.'

Gawd pickle me nut exclamation of surprise; author's *Cityscapes*, 1977: 'Gawd pickle me nut. Lambton Station! Must have had 14 entrances.'

g'day universal Kiwi greeting, also spelled 'gidday'.

geek to peer; Cornish dialect 'geek', to look intently at; eg 'Hey, Mac, let's take a geek at what that joker's up to.' Since WWI.

Gentle Annie an easy slope or a difficult slope; originally a coachman's term.
— a barmaid, specifically Annie Bowling in Queenstown area; ref. James McNeish's *Tavern in the Town*; also the name of a song and a Turkish gun at the Dardanelles, 1915.

get down on to steal; eg 'Let's get down on some of these stereos, eh?' NZA.

get in behind!/ geddinb'hind! legendary farmer's order to his or her dog to move in on sheep or cattle; c/p of Fred Dagg, comedian.

get intercoursed! euphemism for 'get fucked!'; eg 'Can't you see I'm busy. Why don't you go and get intercoursed!'

get Karitanied get pregnant; after Karitane hospitals of the Plunket Society, where new Mums are looked after.

get on it dedicated drinking of alcohol; eg 'Is that you Colin? Hey, what d'ya say we get on it tonight?'

get off the grass! scornful reaction; eg 'You're putting me on. You reckon he'll be All Black fullback before he leaves school? With all the jokers they have for the position? Get off the grass!'

get out from under escape a tricky situation; eg 'If we just hang in and nobody blabs, we should get out from under, if we're lucky.'

get-out set of clothes.

get out of it stoned on marijuana; eg 'I'm bored. You guys want to get out of it tonight?' [*Alison Gray*]

get plunked get pregnant; by association with the Plunket Society, which looks after pregnant mums if required.

get rooted! vigorous objection; eg 'Me play Aussie rules? Ahh. Get rooted!' NZA.

get stuck in! supporter advice to rugby players to become more aggressive or involved; c.1920, migrated to Australia and Britain; eg 'C'mon, Waikato. Get stuck in! Whatareya? Poofters?!'

get to it! urge to act; eg 'Get to it, will you. We haven't got all day.'

get Trubied get pregnant; after Sir Truby King, founder of the Plunket Society.

gink a look; variant of geek. NZA.

give someone curry to abuse or razz vigorously, often in sport; from the heat associated with curry; eg 'That useless Aussie bowler, did we give him some curry!' NZA.

give it a birl/burl make an attempt; from causing the coin to spin in the game of two-up; also **give it a go** and **give it a pop**; eg 'If nobody else will ride the damn horse, I'll give it a birl/go/pop.' Mostly NZA.

give it away to abandon, often in exasperation; eg 'Give it away, Sean, it's just not worth it.' NZA.

give it to the Belgians WWI advice to a comrade complaining of food or gear.

give jaro to scold (Maori 'whauraura', to scold); eg 'If that kid doesn't pipe down soon I'll give it jaro, by crikey.'

give jute to kid or tease; author's *The G'Day Country*, 1985: 'Gave him some jute.'

give somebody their running shoes dismiss from political office; what Governor General Kerr gave Prime Minister Gough Whitlam.

give the go to reject a suitor or abandon a place or job; short for 'give the go-by'; eg 'Why don't we give this game the go, eh?'

glassy a glass marble. NZA.

glide time an attempt by the Public Service to let staff work the 40-hour week that suited them became the title of Roger Hall's blockbuster play and ever since the concept has been informally viewed as an excuse for skiving or working for the government at a pace that would suit the most laid-back snail.

glory box chest containing a young lady's manchester collection in anticipation of marriage; aka 'bottom drawer' and 'hope chest', latter still used in US. NZA.

gnawing kissing, streetkid style; eg 'We did some gnawing, that was it. She didn't want to go any further.' [*Alison Gray*]

go, phr. **it's a go** the deal is on; eg 'G'morning, Cabinet. First, the bad news. Political union with the Aussies is on. It's a go. Now, the good news. It won't happen for years.'

go around with keep steady company with a sexual partner, before or outside of marriage; eg 'Tom's been going around with Jane for six years now. Still hasn't tied the knot.' NZA.

go bite your bum! get lost! You're not wanted here. NZA.

go for one's life give something your complete effort, or encouraged to do so ; eg 'Look, she's alone now, you wimp. Here's your chance. Go for your life.'

go for the doctor again your supreme effort, or betting all your money on one race; the phrase comes from a card game called 'forty-fives', popular on the West Coast from goldmining times, of Irish origin; author's *Ghost Towns of New Zealand*: 'Gambling was poker or 45s, a diggers' game . . . involving legs, queer suits and Maggie, cries of "Get jinx!" and "Go for the doctor!" ' NZA.

go hostile act angrily; eg 'If he says one more word to her, I'll really go hostile.'

go like a cut cat go or depart fast; eg 'Whatever you think of motor scooters, these new Vitas go like a cut cat. True!'

go much on like or care for, usually in negative phr. 'not go much on'; eg 'I don't go much on the new Deputy Head. Do you?'

Probably NZA use first. Recorded Jean Devanny in *Lenore Divine*, 1926.

go off at to abuse, eg 'If she says any more about me behind my back, you have my permission to go off at her hard as you like.' NZA.

go on the swag become a tramp; eg 'During the Great Depression, many men had no choice but to go on the swag. There was nothing for them to do at home.' NZA.

go out with keep company with; eg 'Peter has been going out with Beryl for yonks, must be at least eight months.'

go to the pack to deteriorate; eg 'Since his wife left him for his best mate, Reg has gone rapidly to the pack.' NZA.
— to fail persistently, as recorded in Barry Crump's *A Good Keen Man*, 1960.

go to the pub, Dad! contemptuous teen advice to an adult being square; ref. Partridge *A Dictionary of Catch Phrases*; c. 1970.

go to whoa, from from beginning to end; eg 'I'd like to hear all the sordid details. Everything — from go to whoa.' NZA.

go-ashore three-legged iron pot suspended over fire by early Europeans.

Godzone God's Own Country; also applied to Australia.

going jade off on another army jungle exercise; eg 'Hey, Corp, what's this about us going jade again? Natives restless, eh?'

goldie an impressive or well-regarded object; used by Mrs Elsie Johns in NZ Oral History Unit, Martinborough study.

goob/goobie a gob of spittle or snot; possibly from American slang for mole or pimple, which is from a 'goober', peanut.

good ink agreeable; eg 'He's the good ink, that lad. Heart of gold, slaves his guts out, no trouble to anyone.' Obs.

Good night, McGuinness! a rather final version of the evening farewell salutation, McGuinness not known; eg 'Ah, well, that's one more than my usual quota. That's it, lads. It's good night, McGuinness. See ya in the morning, maybe.' c. 1910.

good-oh exclamation of approval or agreement; variant of right-oh; eg 'Adds up, does it, Mr B? Yes? Good-oh, then. See you next week. Bye.' NZA.

good on ya/yer/you matey expression of approval; eg 'Good on you, sport, you're a bloody bewdy, bringing round the chainsaw. Promise I'll get it back in one or three pieces. No sweat.' NZA.

goog an antipodean egg, often a boiled one; probably from a toddler attempt, or a contraction of 'good egg'.
— an idiot.
Both NZA.

goory Pakeha corruption of 'kuri', Maori for dog, usually used as abusive term for a person, or a dog; eg 'Get that goory off my property quick smart, or I call the cops.'

gorsepocket mean person; phr. **he's got gorse in his pocket**.

Gothic punk dressed entirely in black, with tight-fitting trousers. [*Alison Gray*]

graft work, usually of the hard manual type. NZA.

grafter willing worker. NZA.

Grassgrub, The New Plymouth/Taumarunui and lower South Island railcar, from green colour of carriages.

graunch to misengage gears, producing graunching sound; any sound indicative of mishandling or likely to ruin machinery. NZA.

greenie Conservationist, c.1970. NZA.

greyhound thinly rolled cigarette. NZA.

groppi mocker dressing up, originally to visit Groppi's teashop/hotel in Cairo, WWII; **Groppi's Light Horse** was combatants' name for base troops at Cairo.

grouse excellent; often applied to a fancied woman, possibly derived from desirability of hunting the game bird grouse; eg as in one hoon to another on a passing beauty: 'Grouse sheila, eh? Wouldn't kick her out of bed.' NZA.

grunds/grundies underwear; rhyming slang Reg Grundy/undie. ANZ.

gumdigger/gumpuncher dentist; from diggers for kauri gum.

gummie gumdigger.

gun excellent person or thing; eg a gun motor or a gun guitarist; originally a fast shearer. [Acland] NZA.

gunga vagina or anus, in phrs. 'up your gunga' or 'stick it up your gunga'; ref. Lyn of Tawa on TVNZ *Cancer Line*, 11 November 1987; possibly from ANZ phr. 'bung it in, Gunga Din!', a direction to go ahead, as with pouring concrete.

gurgler plughole, often phr. **down the gurgler** ruined or lost; eg 'There goes another bright idea down the gurgler.' NZA.

gutbuster a mountain likely to bust your gut because so difficult; mostly trampers' term.

gutser glutton. NZA.

gutsful more than enough; phr. **had a gutsful**; eg 'I've had a gutsful of this party. Let's go.'

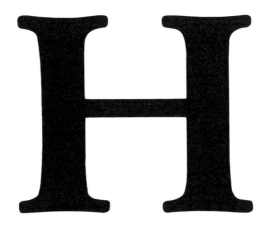

had it totally exhausted or totally exasperated; originally, says Partridge, North Queensland for totalled, or killed; eg 'I've had it, I'm afraid, but you go on' and 'I've had it up to here with you.' ANZ.

half-g flagon of draught beer; shortened form of imperial measure half-gallon.

half-pie half-hearted or poorly performed; probably Maori 'pai', good; eg 'The whole team had been on the booze the night before and were only playing half-pie.'

hand that lifts the cup that cheers, The/Should not be used to shift the gears homily against drinking and driving, especially of farm machinery. [*Shepard*]

handle glass of beer with handle; also **half-handle**; pint and half-pint, in imperial measures.

hang of a/hanguva intensive regarding something big or forceful; euphemistic version of 'helluva'; a fervent intensive favoured by juveniles; eg 'That was a hanguva good flick, eh? NZA.
— **like hang** euphemistic phrase for 'like hell'; eg 'That was a hang of a good movie, eh?' 'Like hang it was!' NZA.

hard case resolute, independent, wild, amusing or sexually available; eg 'Boy, that Morrie's a hard case when it comes to impressing the sheilas. I've never seen him dip out yet.'

hard doer incorrigible person, wag; eg 'Cliff's a hard doer, take my word for it. He's written off 15 stock cars, never won a race, no prize money. Now he's mortgaged his house to get another.' NZA.

hard hitter bowler hat. NZA.

hard shot law unto self, fiercely independent; eg 'Frank's a real hard shot, no question. Lost everything in the fire, wasn't insured, won't accept help from anybody.'

hard thing resolute, outspoken or abrupt loner; eg 'Polt's been up in that old whare for years, never spoken to a soul, except to buy his provisions, when he has to. Hard thing, that Polt.'

hard word, the demand, often for sex, often phr. **put the hard word on**; eg 'Jimmy had been putting the hard word on Helen for years, but she wouldn't come across. It wasn't as if she had them queuing up outside her door, but she had her standards.'

hash-me-gandy sheep station stew; ref. meagre eating habit of Mahatma Gandhi and English 'salmagundi', spiced meat and eggs; c. 1920. NZA.

have on to challenge or attack; WWII; eg 'Have him on about it, he'll back down for sure.'

have up bring before a court; eg 'Have him up over it, he hasn't got a legal leg to stand on.'

hay makes the bull fat response to someone saying 'hey' or 'eh?' instead of 'I beg your pardon'; local variant of 'hay is for horses'.

he, phr. **I'll go he** exclamation of surprise; believed by Partridge from children's game where child blindfolded or otherwise disadvantaged; eg 'If that's not a notornis, I'll go he.' c. 1920.

head, phr. **need your head read** you are insane or stupid; eg 'That's the third time this week you've put on odd socks. You need your head read, you do.' Mostly NZA.

heaps, phr. **give him/her/it heaps** give someone trouble or suggestion that you give something all your effort; eg 'Give her heaps, boy. Go on, that old dunga's used to it.' NZA.

hen cackle a mountain rated easy by climbers; any trifle.

hen fruit hen's eggs. NZA.

hen's teeth, as scarce as extremely scarce. Mostly ANZ.

herbs power/speed ratio, phr. **give him/her/it herbs** or **plenty of herbs** usually suggestion you depress car accelerator to the floor or its maximum; originally sluggish horses were given more herbs, or oats. NZA.

here we sits, like birds in the wilderness rural tranquillity away from urban rat race. [Shepard]

here's a go comment on anticipated happening; eg a run-out in cricket. NZA.

hide insensitive nature or impudent manner, in phrs 'you have a thick hide' or 'you've got a hide'. Mostly NZA.

hickey love bite [Alison Gray]
— thingummygig, late C19.

hiss to tramp rapidly, in phr. **hiss along**; mostly among trampers.

hiss and a roar, with a something done with much noise or fuss; eg 'Jonesy began the marathon with a hiss and a roar, but soon faded.'

hisser term of approval, mostly among trampers, in such contexts as 'a hisser of a day' or 'a hisser of a stew'.

hit your straps to take off quickly; possibly from earlier meaning of looking for one's swag-straps, meaning to consider looking for another job. [Partridge]

hockey sticks hogget chops. [Shepard]

hoe in(to) to do something vigorously, like eating or work; of agricultural origin; eg 'Jack was starving and, without waiting for grace to finish, started hoeing into the hockey sticks.' c. 1920. NZA.

hoick to spit, possibly from its sound, or even from its relation to 'hoick' as jerking, such as at the start and end of a rowing stroke. NZA.

hokianga, a a thick mutton sandwich. [*Shepard*]

Hokitika swindle calling of a certain number in sequence with the aim of creating a jackpot, which is used to buy rounds of drinks in a pub.

hokonui illicitly distilled whisky, from its most notable production in the Hokonui hills of Southland.

holding paddock pensioners' flats or old-age housing settlement; from paddock stock held in on way to slaughterhouse; described by Jim Henderson as 'Wairarapa laconic'.

hollow as a bunghole in a barrel empty or drained.

hollow log dog; rhyming slang, among shearers. ANZ.

hollywood dubious sporting injury demonstrated with transparent acting of a kind associated with Hollywood films; **do a hollywood** perpetrate such dubious acting. NZA.

home nostalgic name for Britain; c.1834. NZA.
— army used for dug-out in the frontline WWI trenches.
— **gone home** worn out clothes.

home and hosed successfully completed; from horse racing; eg 'Looks already like John Walker's home and hosed in the mile.' NZA.

home on the pig's back very successful or easy; eg 'If this horse wins, we're home on the pig's back.' Mostly NZA.

homey dismissive name for a person, usually a migrant, who nostalgically looks to Britain as home.

hoodackie thingummygig; variant of 'doodackie'.

hooer/hua anybody you don't like; literally a whore; appears in Bruce Mason's *The End of the Golden Weather*; Scottish or mock-Scottish; NZ and elsewhere.

hook your mutton clear out, similar to 'slinging your hook'; eg 'Let's hook our mutton, there's no welcome here, fellas.'

hoon hooligan; in pre-WWII Australia, a procurer of prostitutes; possibly German origin. ANZ.

hooning wild or raucous behaviour, often phr. **hooning around**; eg 'After losing the match, the visiting team got drunk and started hooning around town.'

hooray cheerful goodbye; Bennett says modification of 'hurrah'.

hooray fuck! WWII army exclamation, modified to **hooray f-f-forget it**, undoubtedly unmodified again at news of war's end. [*Jim Henderson*]

hooped drunk.

hoot money; corruption of Maori 'utu', ransom or price; also **hootoo, hout** and **hutu**; c. 1840.

hooya! derisive juvenile exclamation; short for 'who are you?'.

hop to it act quickly, command so to do; eg 'Come on now, you lily-livered bunch of nancy boys, when I say the word, hop to it!' NZA.

hop up and down agitated; eg 'When the radio in the TAB went on the blink, the solitary punter with $100 on the nose began to hop up and down like a flea in a fit.'

hophead drunkard and/or crazy person. NZA.

hopped out drunk; Gordon Slatter's *A Gun in My Hand.*

hori mildly derogatory term for a Maori, usually a male one; literally Maori transcription of 'George', one of a number of excuses offered a few years ago to explain the use of the word in Parliament, without however cutting any ice.

hose in win easily; eg 'Free 'n' Easy hosed in, fulfilling the faith of all those punters who had made her odds on favourite for the cup.'

hosed off fed up; perhaps from being hosed with water, just possibly connected with English late-C16 colloquialism 'in my other hose', expressing refusal or disbelief. Current usage would be: 'Was I hosed off when the first decent shower of rain brought down the wooden retaining wall I'd spent a whole day building.'

hospital pass rugby passing of ball to player about to be heavily tackled; eg 'When Gary threw Barry a hospital pass with two dirty big Wallaby flankers converging on him, you could hear the collective gasp of 42,000 spectators over the anguished voice of TV commentator Keith Quinn.'

hostie air hostess.

how much would you charge to haunt a ten-room house? sarcastic rhetorical question to an ugly person.

how's it goin', mate? Kiwi greeting; quintessentially so.

how's the way? colloquial greeting earlier this century.

how ya goin', mate? Kiwi greeting, fairly quintessential.

huckery unwell, jaundiced; possibly developed from Maori 'pakaru', ruined, via its corruption 'huckeroo'.

Hughie God, matily addressed in phr. **send her down, Hughie** a request for rain. ANZ.

huntaway mustering dog; boulder in upper South Island rolled down steep slopes with same mustering purpose. [*Jim Henderson*]

hurl vomit. NZA.

I couldn't care less if the cow calves or breaks its leg expression of not caring; local addition to c/p 'I couldn't care less.'

I didn't come down in the last shower I am not a fool; to which the reply is: 'You mightn't have come down in the last shower, but you're pretty wet all the same.' NZA variant of Royal Navy's 'I didn't come down in the last bucket.'

ickem soft sheep or cow shit, not the hard black hail or dried-out variety, but the stuff in which you can stamp out an indelible footprint. [*Shepard*]

identity local person of some stature, possibly quaint, usually because long-term resident; short for 'old identity'; c.1862. — effete; late last century, when possibly there was no room in those expanding times for old identities.

if you fell off the *Tamahine*, you'd come up with a mouthful of fish said to someone struck lucky; told to Joy Shepard by an Irishwoman.

if your brains was barbed wire, you couldn't fence a dunny you are stupid; Stevan Eldred-Grigg's *Oracles and Miracles*, 1987, of pre-1939 era.

iffy dubious, risky, uncertain; eg 'That bike you bought looks a bit iffy.' c. 1920. Mostly NZA.

I'll hand it to him/I've got to hand it to him recognition of some achievement, to speaker's surprise, often a back-handed compliment; eg 'You've got to hand it to him, he surprised us all winning that race.' c. 1930; also Brit.

I'll see you right typically matey promise to look after someone in trouble or need; eg 'Don't worry, mate, I'll see you right for money.' [*Jim Henderson*]

in you go, says Bob Munro an encouraging c/p. NZA.

Inch and Pinch Peninsula of Gallipoli; soldiers 1915.

influence in the right quarter latrine or other menial duty; ironic WWI army.

it's a little bit over the false plea of many an antipodean butcher, carrying the unspoken rider: 'Do you mind, dear?'

I've got a carbuncle on me pollywonkle facetious reply to enquiry about what's wrong, usually from a question-happy kid.

I've nearly bust my foofer I have overexerted and almost ruptured something; foofer probably 'foofoo' or 'poopoo valve', the mythical gadget the Royal Navy blames for anything that goes wrong. [*Shepard*]

jack a look; eg 'Let's take a jack at this new bowler, eh?'
— to organise or prepare; eg 'I'll leave you to jack this crew, Jill, and I'll take the rest.'
— **jack of** rid of or weary of; eg 'Would I like to be jack of those little twerps!' c. 1890. NZA.
— **jack up** to fix or renovate; eg 'Can you jack up billets?'
— to prop up; from a car jack; eg 'If we can jack up this fence it might last a few more years.' NZA.
— to raise, as in prices and wages; eg 'I see this bloody government's jacked up taxes again.' NZA.
— to be framed or put in trouble or deceived; from double-headed penny

known as a 'jack' in the game of two-up; eg 'It's pretty obvious it's a jack up between the two leaders.'

jackberko quail in Central Otago; from the sound it makes.

Jacky Howe navy or black sleeveless woollen singlet worn by labourers; after champion shearer. ANZ.

jagged tired in trampers' terminology; also depressed or irritating.

jam and butter it! as mild a curse as 'darn it!', but can be used in mild or mean situation; Shepards suggest you are in a tearing hurry to catch a waiting bus, you grab the supposedly locked cashboxes, one in each hand, and head for the safe, and the lid comes open on one, out falls a trail of coins . . .; a milder example: the cook says, 'Oh, jam and butter it, I forgot the spice!'

jandals thongs; brand name.

jar glass of beer; NZA; Brit. use for a drink of beer.

Jessie's dream methylated spirits; Isaiah 11:1: 'And there shall come forth a rod out of the stem of Jesse'; WWII army. [*Jim Henderson*]

Jimmy Grant an immigrant; rhyming slang of whalers, recorded by Edward Jerningham Wakefield in *Adventure in New Zealand*, 1845.

jingle money; probably from sound coins make in pocket; c.1925. NZA.

jingling johnnies hand shears, the shearer a **jingling johnny**; c.1870. ANZ.

jink to swindle; originally to take all the tricks in a game of 'forty-fives'; c.1920. NZA.

joe a fool, or acting foolishly, in phr. **make a joe of yourself**; from derisive use of word to identify police in Victorian goldfields mid-C19. ANZ.

joe hunt a foolish person; rhyming slang with 'cunt'.

john Chinese, from mid-C19 goldminers calling them John Chinamen. ANZ.
— penis; short for 'John Thomas'. Mostly ANZ.
— policeman; from 'John Hop/cop' rhyming slang. ANZ and Brit.

John Dillon a shilling; rhyming slang, c.1930, but also name of a well-known racehorse.

johnny-come-lately new arrival; disapproving term; originally a farm hand just out from England, c.1910. ANZ.

Johnny Woodser lone drinker in a pub, Kiwi variant of 'Jimmy Woodser', Australian who gave his name to the solitary occupation.

jug large glass or plastic jug in which public bars have in recent decades dispensed a litre of beer at a time.

jumbo backside, c.1945.
[*Partridge*]

just quietly confidential
aside, WWI; eg 'Just
quietly, this is the best
steak I've ever had.' NZA.

just the job exactly what
you want; eg 'Good on
you, cobber, that's just the
job for a man with a
thirst.' NZA.

kai food; from Maori to eat or drink anything other than water; used WWI soldiers, while Australian soldiers preferred Melanesian pidgin 'kaikai', meaning food.

kaikart fast food takeaway or piecart.

Karitane, a a Plunket nurse, trained member of the Plunket Society, the Royal New Zealand Society for the Health of Women and Children, founded by Sir Truby King in 1907 at his Karitane home near Dunedin. (He called his society after the then Governor General.)

Karitane yellow hideous yellow paint associated with Plunket hospitals.

kath indefinite term of imprisonment; originally the duration of WWI; from *Kathleen Mavourneen*, early-C19 song by one Miss Crawford, with words: 'It may be for years and it may be forever.' NZA.

keep your shirt on advice not to lose your temper or be so impatient, from habit of removing shirt before fighting, eg 'Okay, keep your shirt on, I didn't mean it.' NZA, also US.

keg beer; from a barrel of beer.

kerbstone jockey a safe job; originally a soldier in transport in WWI, with his horse heavily harnessed.

kia ora! hello; from Maori 'good health!'; Reed/Karetu *Concise Maori Dictionary*, 1984.

kidney pie insincere praise; WWI. NZA.

kidney rotter frameless backpack, giving trampers' kidneys a hard time; aka **kidney buster/crusher/ sweater/rider**.

'kin oath rude avowal; contraction of 'fucking oath'; eg 'That was a bastard of a stump to dig out.' ''Kin oath, mate. 'Kin oath.' NZA.

KISS! Keep It Simple, Stupid! Army acronym.

kitchen tea female version of stag party on eve of wedding, usually not especially alcoholic and usually where sensible kitchen or domestic presents are given to the bride-to-be. NZA.

Kiwi New Zealander, c.1917; specifically, name for New Zealand rugby league players and athletes when representing their country at international gatherings; self-awarded nickname of hearty 1960s Prime Minister Keith 'Call me Kiwi' Holyoake; originally and still Maori name for the flightless New Zealand bird that has become our national emblem.

knockabout handyman, or station hand from c.1875. NZA.

knock back rejection or refusal, often of sex; eg 'He systematically propositioned every woman at the party, and was knocked back every time.' NZA.

knock down to drain a glass of a beverage, usually alcoholic, mostly beer; eg 'He knocked down the yard of ale and called for another.'
— to spend freely, particularly on drink. NZA.
— introduction; in Frank S. Anthony's *Me and Gus*.

knocker, phr. **on the knocker** punctual; originally 'cash on the knocker', meaning cash on demand, prompt payment required; eg 'Crombie is invariably here on the knocker for council meetings, no matter how busy he might be.' NZA.

komaty dead or wounded soldier, WWI, later referring to a horse; from Maori 'Ka mate', 'First was death!', the opening lines of Te Rauparaha's famous haka celebrating deliverance from his enemies, now chanted by the All Blacks before doing test battle, by the national rugby league team if they have won a test battle.

kotanga car aerial; current racist pun on English word 'coathanger'.

kumara cruncher a Maori; offensive.

la/lala toilet; euphemistically short for lavatory.

Lady of October clematis.

land of the wrong white crowd New Zealand perceived as dominated by Pakehas, backlash c/p variant of translation of Maori name for New Zealand, 'Aotearoa', land of the long white cloud.

larrikin rowdy youth; of several possible origins, including Warwickshire or Worcestershire dialect 'larrikin', a mischievous youth, Macquarie choice; Baker suggests word travelled from antipodes to Britain; Partridge acknowledges originally mostly antipodes, thinks most likely origin Cornish 'larrikin', a person who larks about; Partridge also favours Larry, popular Irish contraction of Lawrence, plus 'kin'. NZA.

laughing gear mouth; eg 'Wrap your laughing gear around this,' says Barry Crump, handing over a gutted fish in a TV ad, 1987.

layby small deposit securing goods from sale until depositor pays the balance (usually progressively) and uplifts the goods; generally operated by drapers and department stores.

leather lady petrified possum skin plastered to a tunnel wall by a passing train; ref. author's *The G'Day Country*.

lemonfish euphemism for shark in fish and chip shops.

lemon-squeezer peaked Kiwi infantry hat, still worn in ceremonial parades.

let her rip get something going, often machinery such as car engine; eg 'Hang on the brakes with the revs up, then let her rip.' NZA.

let me chat you allow me to tell you something, WWI Anzac c/p.

let the hare sit ease up, take it easy; Jim Henderson traces to Timaru.

lick an ice cream, among 1960s teens.

lick at the cat and a run round the table, a the serving of a meagre meal or the suggestion that you have eaten very little. [*Shepard*]

lickety spit very fast, in a great hurry; local variant of US 'lickety split'.

like a dog golloping tripe sexual intercourse; Southland saying.

like a fart in a fit in hopeless if not desperate trouble; eg 'He ran from room to room, like a fart in a fit.' [*Jim Henderson*]

like a fart on a curtain pole in a great hurry. [*Shepard*]

like a hooer at a christening confused milling; eg 'The starting gun failed to go off and left the yachts dodging each other like hooers at a christening.' [*Jim Henderson*] ANZ.

like a maggot on a hot plate incessant wriggling about; eg 'After three hours of listening to *Die Walküre* on the hideously uncomfortable wooden seats, he was beside himself with restlessness, like a maggot on a hot plate.' [*Jim Henderson*]

like talking to a brick wall you are not listening to me.

lip like a motherless foal youngster accused of sulking or pouting; eg 'There's no point in putting on that face. My, my, Missy, you've got a lip there like a motherless foal.' [*Jean Henderson*]

liquid laugh vomit. ANZ.

little house, the toilet. NZA.

little lady, the the wife; a patronising hubby word; eg 'And how is the little lady after a day slaving over a hot microwave?' NZA.

lizard sheep musterer, by association with shearing handpiece of same name. — idler; short for 'lounge lizard', a lounge bar idler after women. Both ANZ.

lolly any sweets, short for lollipop. NZA. — **chuck** or **lose your lollies** to spew. — **do one's lolly** lose one's temper. NZA.

lolly scramble children rucking for sweets. — any unseemly pursuit of power, often applied to political promises at election time.

lolly water soft drink or weak alcoholic drink. NZA.

long john oblong loaf of bread baked in tin container.

long paddock roadside, where free grazing available. NZA.

loopies tourists; dismissive term by locals, possibly because tourists do a quick loop and off.

lunatic soup alcoholic drink, including meths (methylated spirits). NZA.

lunch box bum, in phr. **open your lunch box**, to fart, aka **drop your lunch box**. NZA.

lungbuster cigarette.

lurk job, plan, ruse, hiding place, hangout (also Brit.); a frequent example: 'You're on to a good lurk', meaning a cushy job; c. 1916. NZA.

lux to vacuum; short for electrolux, used to puzzling effect on English immigrants in Roger Hall play *Prisoners of Mother England*; **lux the Venetians** vacuum clean the Venetian blinds.

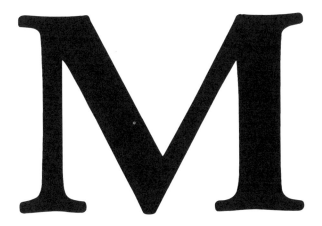

mad as a maggot very mad, very silly, very angry, very eccentric; Gordon Slatter; eg 'Old Millie's mad as a maggot, you know, hosing the lawn when it's raining, that sort of thing.'

mad as a meataxe very mad, very angry. NZA.

mad as a wet hen very angry and very silly simultaneously.

mad-dogging to pester; eg 'Don't mad-dog me, boy, can't you see I'm concentrating.'

mad money splurge money; originally return ship fare WWI soldiers believed English girls brought with them in case their Kiwi soldier boy went mad, ie acted with excessive freedom. [*Baker*]

Mainland, The the South Island, self-declared.

makan food, from Malay verb 'to eat', ingested by army.

mai mai makeshift shelter of sticks and grass employed by Maori, latterly duckshooters' hide; Macquarie identifies as Aboriginal, yet not used in Australia.

make a box of make a mess of; eg 'He was going well in his first woodchop, until he got distracted by sweat in one eye, missed his groove and made a box of it.' NZA.

71

make a break run away from the police, c.1932. [*Partridge*] ANZ.

malt sandwich a beer; used Mark Leishman, *Today Tonight*, TVNZ, 2 September 1987.

mango Kiwi $50 note; because note is orange, like the fruit; often used in card games like poker for high stakes.

Maori bunk common bed for several people, usually trampers; not intended to be insulting.

maorihead aka 'niggerhead' or *Carex secta*, a tussocky plant in swamps that looks, when burned off, like a blackened head.

Maori overdrive sliding your car in neutral downhill; offensive.

Maori PT taking a rest; jokey, offensive.

Maori roast a pie and a jug; offensive.

Maori sidestep headlong knees-threshing barge through a tackle; doubly offensive.

Maori time as much time as desired; easygoing.

massive! adolescent exclamation of approval; eg 'That party the other night, massive, eh!'

mate's rates payment that may not involve the Inland Revenue department, usually for trade work, not necessarily involving mates; eg 'I can work on your boat weekends. Strictly cash. Mate's rates, eh?'

MDO Maori day off; a sickie, or a day absent from work with pretended illness; offensive.

meat tickets identity discs worn on neck and wrist, WWII. [*Jim Henderson*]

mechanised dandruff crabs or body lice active in pubic region, first identified so by WWII soldiers. [*Jim Henderson*]

med heads military police; current army slang.

Melbourne cup chamber pot, after the famous horse race first run 1861.

metho methylated spirits addict. NZA.

Mickey Doolan Roman Catholic and usually Irish, aka **mick, mickey, Mickey Doo**; 'mick' used elsewhere.

milkbar cowboy a post-war bikie, though probably not anymore. NZA.

mimi hill comfort stop; from Maori 'mimi', to urinate; eg 'Coming up to mimi hill, chief?'

minge-muncher enthusiast for cunnilingus.

mocker bellbird, from Maori 'mako-mako'.
— clothing; **mockered up** dressed up, specifically from 1935 woman's dress; used by Gordon Slatter: 'Have you seen that trot [woman] in the blue mocker?' Possibly Romany word 'mockodo' or 'mockeedo', filthy, used ironically to mean opposite. NZA.

mockers bad luck, in phr. **put the mockers on**, from Yiddish for 'bad luck'; originally one of the 10 plagues. NZA.

mockie bellbird.

moke an inferior horse, or jocular reference to a horse, as in Frank S. Anthony's *Me and Gus*; elsewhere a donkey or ass. NZA.

moleskin squatter working man who has acquired a small sheep run; from his moleskin trousers. NZA.

Mondayitis the blues, depression, particularly at the prospect of having to work; from the day after the weekend, when this condition is most apparent. NZA.

mong mongrel; also popular as a mild term of abuse. NZA.

monte a certainty, often in reference to a likely winner; from the three-card monte trick of Spanish American card game; eg 'Put your money on Bluebell in the Fifth, she's a monte.'
— a fine person or thing, by extension; eg 'Old Claude's a monte, he'd do anything for you.'
Both NZA.

more jungletime up than Tarzan a lot of time spent in the field; army slang.

Morepork, The North Auckland train, from its melancholy whistle in the night.

mountain oysters lamb testicles, for some a gourmet delight.

mountain mop
Dracophyllum traversii plants
used by trampers in
Canterbury area as cleaner
for pots and billies. (Cf
Tararua dishmop.)

move out to bloom or
expand; eg 'Since he
promoted himself to
opening bat, Jeff has really
moved out and put his
batting woes behind him.'

multi short for multi-
millionaire; mostly
Auckland; eg 'Were you at
Michael's Speight Road
house warming? No? You
wouldn't read about it.
Nothing but multis, as far
as the eye could see.'

mungas/munja Kiwi
version of 'mungey',
Services slang for 'food';
possibly from French
'manger', to eat, possibly
borrowed in Crimean War;
Gordon Slatter writes of
WWII 'munja party'.

muster an easy beat a
comfy job (Jim
Henderson); eg 'Here's me
pulling night patrols and
you're pen pushing. You
mustered an easy beat,
mate.'

mutton penis. NZA.

muttonfish paua.

muttonflaps labia majora.

my arse is a red cabbage
c/p indicative of total
confidence; eg 'If he jumps
over two metres, my arse
is a red cabbage.'

my colonial oath! a mild
expletive used usually as
reinforcement, with
variations such as **my
oath!, my bloody oath!, my
bloody colonial oath!**
NZA.

my elbow! exclamation of
surprise or disbelief, used
by Frank S. Anthony in
Me and Gus, perhaps as a
variation of 'my eyes!'

naked lady pink orchid found Australasia.

Narg an Indian; offensive.

native chewing gum puha stalk used for chewing, bitter at first, good mixed with resin from tarata or lemonwood or the leaves of the rangiora.

neato pleasing; variant of 'neat', as in **neat, eh?**

Nelson snob a person from Nelson.

nest of sparrows flew out of me arse, a I am sexually satisfied. 'Immortal', Jim Henderson rates this c/p.

new chum novice or new arrival; originally on goldfields, as dismissive as American term 'greenhorn'. ANZ.

new iniquity immigrants, specifically from Australia to the Otago goldrush areas, 1860s to 1880s; the opposite of 'old identity'.

New Zild New Zealand the way others hear us say it, allegedly through gritted teeth.

Ngati Drongo not our tribe! eg 'Was that your lot involved in the Maori Loans Affair?' 'Nah. That was Ngati Drongo.' [*Tom Scott*]

nick away to leave, usually surreptitiously or quickly; eg 'Look, I'm going to nick away before the speeches start. Let me know if they say anything important, will you?'

nick over to visit, usually without warning; eg 'Marge, I'm just going to nick over and see Harry before din-dins, okay?'

ningnong idiot, in variation of Northern English dialect 'ning-nang'; also a worthless person or horse; eg 'What a bloody ningnong Percy turned out to be. Just shows some qualifications aren't worth the paper they're printed on.' NZA.

Nippon clipon the extra lanes on the outside of the Auckland harbour bridge, Japanese-made and attached without piles to existing structure.

no sense sticking your nose in butter if you're going to have to eat dripping the rest of your life a discouragement to put on airs if you cannot afford them, usually parental negativity towards offspring leaving the nest in Depression era, as quoted in Stevan

Eldred-Grigg's *Oracles and Miracles*. (Longest c/p known to compiler.)

nobody home not concentrating; a vacant mind; eg 'I asked him why he did it, but I might as well have saved my breath, there's nobody home.'

nohi nosey person, often **Jack nohi**; from Maori 'kanohi', the face; eg 'You bloody nohi, why don't you get on with your own work and leave me to do mine in peace and quiet.'

no-hoper totally incompetent or inadequate person socially or at sport; used in horse racing for a useless racehorse; eg 'Cripes, that horse is a no-hoper: six starts, and last in every one.' c. 1925. NZA.

no worries expression of confidence; eg 'Even without Martin Crowe we're a match for the Aussies, no worries.' NZA.

nobbler mid-C19 dram of any alcoholic spirit, usually gin, whisky, rum or brandy. NZA.

North Sea rabbit herrings to WWI soldiers.

nong idiot; short for 'ningnong'; eg 'I tell you, Pasmore is a complete and utter nong. You only have to look at the stupid way he walks.' NZA.

nose, phr. **a bit on the nose** protest at unfairness; eg 'Hey, no spitting, okay? Come on, that's a bit on the nose. Fair dos, eh?' NZA.

not really shifty way of saying no; eg 'Do you know where Mein Street is?' 'Not really.'
— also used ironically to signal scepticism.

not the full quid not sound in the head; eg 'There's no doubt in my mind, he's not the full quid. I mean, who else laughs every time there's a quiet moment in the service?' NZA.

nuddy phr. **in the nuddy** cute way of saying nude; eg 'Please Miss, we saw Sandra swimming down the riverhole in the nuddy. We did!' NZA.

nuggeting unpleasant male party habit of removing victim's trousers and underpants and applying Nugget shoe polish to testicles; eg 'Let's get him pissed then give him a good nuggeting. Show the stuck-up prick we don't need his hoitytoity ways round here. Whadya say?'

Number Eight the best, strongest, most likely to succeed; from the thick gauge No. 8 fencing wire used on farms; eg Joy Shepard remembers a doctor saying to a patient on whom he had done surgery that had come a bit unstuck: 'I'll use No.8 this time and make a real job of it.'

nut, the rugby ball.

OE overseas experience, the young Kiwi's working holiday abroad, mandatory and meaningful; coined by John Muirhead and popularised in late 1970s by friend and columnist Tom Scott; in 1980s, title of Keith Ovenden novel.

off one's face stoned on marijuana; eg 'Only had a few puffs of that new stuff, eh. Off my face. Yeh.' [*Alison Gray*]

offsider assistant, hanger-on, friend, partner, all or some of these; originally assistant to bullock driver, walking on the offside of the team; eg 'I see Hart's offsider is now coaching the team.' NZA.

oil, the the truth, the information you need, an excellent person or thing; eg 'Phil had the oil all right on Brierleys. Sold all he had the day before the bottom fell out of the market.'

oh, bloody good, whacko, Pup! Kiwi war cry after downing Japanese plane WWII; Partridge, *A Dictionary of Catch Phrases.*

okay, lah intensified agreement, army slang using Malay 'lah', a suffix supplying emphasis; eg 'You boys stick with your friendly neighbourhood sergeant, this'll be a piece of piss. Okay?' 'Yeh, Sarge. Okay, lah!'

old identity long-term resident, popularised by goldfields balladeer Charles Thatcher, coined by E.B. Cargill in Otago Provincial Council when he said early settlers should endeavour to preserve their old identity amidst all these 1860s new goldrush identities.

old man a rural object of striking or large appearance; eg old man paddock or old man rock. NZA.

olds parents; eg 'What's the big attraction with dope, anyway? Most of the olds smoke it.' NZA.

on it drinking alcohol; eg 'I'm sick of footy practice. Let's get on it instead, eh?' NZA.

on the bash an alcoholic drinking bout, particularly in New Zealand and Scotland; eg 'I feel ghastly. I was on the bash most of the night.'

on the scoot drinking spree; eg 'I'm surprised he's still upright, let alone at work. I hear he's been on the scoot every night this week.' NZA.

once more round the gasworks one more effort, please; eg 'C'mon, fellas, we're just about finished. Once more round the gasworks, eh?' [Shepard]

one star artist second lieutenant, WWI.

oozle to obtain illicitly or by scheming. WWI.

op shop opportunity or secondhand shop, often selling clothes cheaply.

open out behaving badly, as in Frank S. Anthony's Me and Gus.

open slather unconstrained and often riotous gathering available to allcomers; possibly from Irish 'slighe', access; eg 'It's open slather, I hear, at the golf clubrooms this Saturday. Coming?' NZA.

ordinary bloke/joker the typical working man, generally held to be possessed of good sense and no nonsense, nor frills, neither; eg 'Crumpy's one of your genuine ordinary jokers, whadya reckon?'

Otago cockney nickname for person from Otago province.

Other Side, The

Australia, the other side of the water; c.1880.

out on its own, like a country shithouse

excellent or unique; eg 'Television has introduced some startling logos over the years, but this one is out on its own, like a country shithouse.' c. 1910.

out to it

unconscious, often from too much alcohol; eg 'Clive wanted to continue with the pub crawl, but Keith was out to it.' NZA.

outer

phr. **on the outer** out of favour, perhaps rejected, or penniless; from the outer enclosure at a racecourse; eg 'After Dick was seen in the big anti-apartheid march on telly, he was on the outer at the rugby club.'

over the fence

unacceptable behaviour, which Partridge thinks from local rules for cricket; eg 'Attacking the Finance Minister in Parliament was one thing, but burning his book in front of the television cameras was, for most of his colleagues, a bit over the fence.'

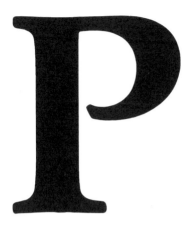

pack a sad to be depressed; from builders' term for a warp; eg 'Having dropped the ball with the line and the winning of the game in sight, Mick proved the night's party pooper, packing a sad all evening.' NZA.

pack shit to be afraid; eg 'Man, when those bikies arrived all at once, skull jackets and shades and all, we packed shit, no two ways about it.' NZA.

packet from Paris a baby; eg 'Hello, dear. As you can see, I'm your Plunket nurse. And what have we here, a dear little packet from Paris. Isn't he gorgeous?' NZA.

paddle pop ice-block; 1960s teen rhyming slang.

pain in the puku a bellyache or irritating person; Maori 'puku', stomach; eg 'That Pom's a pain in the puku.'

pakapoo ticket, look/ marked like a something confusing or incomprehensible; from Chinese lottery ticket with its (to Europeans) incomprehensible markings. Housie-type game played in illegal gambling and opium dens such as those in Haining Street, Wellington; eg 'This ruddy exam's marked like a pakapoo ticket!' NZA.

Pakeha Williams defines as a person of predominantly European descent. Other meanings include an imported variety of kumara, a silver eel, a flea, while 'pakepakeha, pakepakeha' are imaginary beings resembling men, with fair skins. Baker ponders possible links with Hebrew 'kehah' meaning 'pale' or 'dim', added to the causative 'pa'; the flea the European introduced to New Zealand; the imported pig or 'poaka'. Dr Johnson is said to have said it was 'a term of endearment amongst sailors', which Morris supports. Partridge opines a Maori word meaning 'fairy' or 'bugger'. Pakeha people adopted the word colloquially about 1850, the singular used but the plural more general, both upper and lower case. Baker identifies the 'pake-has' or wealthy white and the 'pake-hasn't' or poor white. Word currently becoming capitalised and controversial.

pakehatanga emerging word for cultural attitudes and origins of European and/or Pakeha New Zealanders.

paki/pakihi bald patch on a man's head, from Maori word 'pakihi' for a natural clearing in the bush.

pannikin boss foreman on building and other jobs; originally manager of a sheep station. ANZ.

paper collared swell white collar worker, usually a clerk, probably **collar proud**: in Alexander Bathgate's *Colonial Expressions*.

pat, phr. **on one's pat** single-handed or alone, short for rhyming slang 'on one's Pat Malone/alone' or on your 'own'; eg 'Since Mabel passed on, Ron's been on his pat far too much. Time we went round and jollied him up, fellas. Agree?' ANZ.

pav pavlova; once the national dessert both sides of Tasman and still subject of debate over which country invented it. A draw is fair, given that David Burton's *Two Hundred Years of New Zealand Food and Cookery* credits a Melbourne woman with creating it for visiting Russian ballerina Anna Pavlova in 1926, the same year a recipe appeared in *Home*

Cookery in New Zealand called 'meringue with fruit filling', the word 'pavlova' appearing here in 1927. Further to this, the *Macquarie Dictionary* awards Australian chef Herbert Sachse the invention, but in 1935, the name coming from Harry Nairn, Esplanade Hotel, Perth. Kiwifruit has probably replaced passionfruit as favoured topping on both sides of Tasman. NZA.

pavs and savs pavlovas and saveloys, the once typical serving at Kiwi gatherings.

pearler superb person or thing; eg 'Thanks for helping out, Sam. You're a bloody pearler, mate.' ANZ.

pepperpotting Maori Affairs past housing policy of sprinkling Maori families among Pakeha ones.

perform to throw a tantrum; eg 'If that kid doesn't get his own way, does he perform! Needs a tickle up, I'd say.' NZA.

peter half-gallon jar.

pickle my daisies! exclamation of doubt; eg 'Pickle my daisies if that's true.' [*Shepard*]

picnic problem; ironic, reversal of what is usually a pleasant occasion; eg 'If you take the boat out in that weather, mate, it's your picnic.' NZA.

pie good, **pie on** expert or efficient, good at, from Maori 'pai', good, 'pai ana', suitable; eg 'That paint job was pie on, ta muchly.'

pig flagon of beer.

pig's arse/bum/ear derisive exclamations; eg 'In a pig's arse to that notion, mate.' NZA.

Pig Islander New Zealander, by association with pigs Captain Cook introduced; no connection with Sir Robert Muldoon's nickname, Piggy, which was coined by Steve Whitehouse in a university revue in early 1960s at Victoria University.

pig out to overindulge; eg 'I could pig out all day on these pavs.'

pike on to let down; eg 'Hal had the caterers in and a ton of booze, huge waste, half his mates piked on him.'

pike out to depart, usually from lusty drinking session, to disapproval of those continuing, but also any agreed activity or deal; eg 'Don't pike out now, Reg, the fun's just starting.' NZA.

pikkie a picture, photographic or cinematic; eg 'Got the holiday pikkies back yet, Marge?' NZA.

pill, the rugby ball. NZA.

pimp to sneak or tell-tale; eg 'There was no doubt how they had got caught; everybody knew Cyril was the class pimp.' NZA.

piss any alcohol; eg 'Nice drop of piss, Fred.' NZA.

piss all over easily beat the competition; eg 'We pissed all over Marist, even though they had that Junior All Black joker.' NZA.

piss awful very unpleasant; eg 'The party was piss awful.' NZA.

piss easy very easy; eg 'The exam was piss easy.'

piss in achieve with consummate ease; eg 'Reckon I'll piss in with this line-up for the 100 metres.'

piss in someone's pocket attempt to ingratiate; eg 'If you want to get in the team you'll just have to piss in his pocket.' NZA.

piss in the hand something easily achieved; eg 'That cross-harbour swim was a piss in the hand.'

piss in the wind self-defeating activity; eg 'You're pissing in the wind trying to beat him on his own turf.' NZA.

piss on regardless continue drinking without considering consequences; eg 'Whether you stay or not, we intend to piss on regardless.'

piss up large abandoned drinking of alcohol; eg 'What do you say we forget about her, mate, and piss up large.'

piss weak inadequate or mean or cowardly; eg 'That halfback is piss weak, guarantee it. One good tackle on him and the game's as good as ours.' NZA.

pisser the pub; eg 'Who's coming down the pisser?' NZA.

pisshead heavy drinker; possibly first in NZ, earlier C20, says Partridge; eg 'You guys are nothing but a bunch of permanent pissheads.'

pissy-eyed drunk, but probably mildly so; eg 'Bert had only had two Steinies and already he felt pissy-eyed. Probably still had a skinful from the night before.'

plate refreshments contributed to a gathering, usually homemade cakes or sandwiches or sausage rolls or savs or pavs, usually by women, hence phr. 'Gents $5, Ladies a plate.' NZA.

play the piano run fingers across sheep backs to find best place to shear, or to detect defects in wool. [Acland]

player person, usually female, prepared to play at sex; c.1950; eg 'I reckon that one in the corner would be a player. Want to find out?'

plonk any alcohol, usually cheap wine, usually nasty; originally cheap pink port sold by quart throughout Australasia in mid-1920s; possibly from 'vin blanc', French for ordinary white wine, as WWI Anzacs perhaps mispronounced it. — to put something down heavily or clumsily or casually; eg 'Plonk that crate over there, mate, sit yourself down and have a snort.'

plum jam lamb; rhyming slang among shearers.

plurry bloody; pidgin in Australia and New Zealand; Partridge says it is from Aboriginal's natural use of the word, OEDS says NZA slang, Turner thinks it a convention of journalists rather than Maori, in support of which was the slanguage of the character Hori in the bestselling book *The Half-Gallon Jar*.

pluty wealthy, but worse, perceived as assuming airs and graces above the level of the egalitarian Kiwi herd; refers also to suburbs that fancy themselves, such as Fendalton in Christchurch, Khandallah or Karori ('We are the Park Lane of New Zealand' overheard comment in London of a woman from Karori) in Wellington, Remuera in Auckland; comes from 'plutocracy', the land barons of the South Island last century.

pole to steal, c.1930, Australia later, but earlier Australian meaning to scrounge.

polish, a fellatio; eg 'Whadya want, sailor, all the way or just a polish?'

Pom/Pommie British immigrant; possibly first used by Sydney wharf workers late C19 as rhyming slang with 'pomegranate', which rhymingly derived from 'Jimmy Grant', whaling slang for immigrant, in Baker's view; Partridge suggests a corruption of 'Tommy', which came back from Boer War; Orsman suggests a reference to sunburned faces. Xavier Herbert wrote in 1963 of saying as children: 'Immigrants, pomegranates, pommies!'

Pomeranian a Pom, fancifully extended by association with mythical Middle European country.

pongo British person; originally used by British sailors to describe marine or soldier they were required to join forces with in WWI, probably not unaware that the word meant 'monkey', though derivation credited to forage cap resembling that worn by the dog Pongo in a Punch and Judy show; brought back by Anzacs as name for their British counterpart.

Pongolia Britain, modelled on Mongolia, promoted successfully by WWII soldier Les Cleveland, who told author he regretted 'Pongoloid' never caught on in the same way.

ponk stink; possibly from Maori 'puhonga', stinking or offensive, and English word 'pong', which has the rare form 'ponk'.

pony smallest glass of beer served in pubs in imperial measure times, usually 5 ounce here and Sydney, 4 ounce other places in Australia; originally American for small glass of liquor.

poohpooh rifle or big gun, WWI; probably Maori 'pu', a piped instrument and a gun.

poon loner, idiot; possibly Aboriginal, possible link English public school word meaning to be unsteady, from Latin 'ponere', to place. NZA.

poo-pusher active male homosexual. NZA.

poozling scavenging in abandoned buildings before the demolisher gets there, old bottles favoured, but anything of antique significance or value.

pop, phr. **have a pop at** a fight; NZA.
— **to go off pop** to start speaking angrily.
— **not a fair pop** not a fair chance; eg 'I'd like to have a pop at the little basket, but I apologise for going off pop at you. It's not a fair pop you having to be involved.' c. 1925.

popular as shit at a nightmen's picnic unpopular; A.R.D. Fairburn Letters, 1981.

porangi mad, eccentric, stupid; eg 'Hey, there's a joker in the public bar's gone completely porangi.' Maori adopted colloquialism late C19.

pork/porking male engagement in sexual intercourse; eg 'I wouldn't say no to porking that one.' Also US.

pork chop, phr. **like a pork chop in a synagogue** inappropriate or ill at ease; eg 'That umpire's about as popular with the Kiwis as a pork chop in a synagogue.' NZA.

pork sword penis; eg 'Exercise the old pork sword last night, did you, Batesy?' NZA and US.

possie useful position or hideaway, developed in dug-outs at Gallipoli; eg 'That's a good possie you've got there for watching the birds from.' NZA.

pot to put a child on the potty. NZA.
— phr. **put someone's pot on** to finish somebody or expose; ref. Frank S. Anthony's *Me and Gus;* c. 1945.

pot-stirrer political or social activist adjudged to enjoy upsetting the status quo; eg 'That Minto's a real pot-stirrer, eh?' NZA.

poultice a large sandwich using everything in the fridge or pantry, akin to American dagwood without the toothpicks; eg 'Looks like you've got the whole deli in that poultice, dear. Don't bolt it down, will you, or it'll be back to see you tonight.'

prat to talk to someone; perhaps from English C19 colloquialism 'praty', talkative, from Southern English 'prate', idle talk; mostly NZA.

Pressbutton Presbyterian; eg 'Look out, you jokers, here come the Pressbuttons!' NZA.

pricey high priced; eg 'Her dresses are good but a bit pricey.' Here c.1910, Brit. since c.1940.

pricker , phr. **get the pricker with** to be angry with; ref. Gordon Slatter; eg 'Watch out, mate. The Sarge has really got the pricker with you.' c. 1930. NZA.

prickhead term of abuse, usually male, often affectionate; eg 'Okay, prickhead, let's play some tennis.'

Proddy dog Protestant, offensive, usually from Catholic children, inviting counter-insult 'Catholic dogs stink like frogs'.

Prophets, The Australian squatters in Canterbury, 1851.

pubbing to drink in pub or series of pubs, aka **pub crawl**; eg 'You guys on for pubbing s'arvo?' NZA.

puckeroo ruin, Maori 'pakaru', broken or shattered to pieces, used WWI soldiers; eg 'This torch is puckerooed!'

pull finger command to hurry up; eg 'Right, let's pull finger and see if we can catch the fleet.' Contraction of English phr. 'pull one's finger out'.

pull someone's tit to make a fool of or tease; eg 'Take it easy, Moss. Can't you see he's just pulling your tit?' NZA.

pull your head in advice to mind one's own business; eg 'I'd prefer to handle this my way. Why don't you just pull your head in?' Partridge traces to army men sticking heads out of troop trains and being advised to pull them in lest they be mistaken for cattle; c. 1930. ANZ.

punch out to beat up; eg 'I intend to punch out that so-and-so.'

punga penis, by association with the tree fern, Maori 'ponga'.
— **how's your punga?** a male student 1960s salutation; eg 'G'day, Bosh, me old cobber. How's ya punga?'

push shit uphill attempt the impossible; eg 'Bringing on replacements won't help, you'd still be pushing shit uphill against that lot.' NZA.

push a turd uphill with a toothpick army version of preceding.

put a shit on to denigrate or deceive; eg 'Look, Pat's a past master at this, he really put a shit on you, no sweat.' NZA.

put an iron on your shoulder get into debt or become beholden to somebody; Stevan Eldred-Grigg, *Oracles and Miracles.*

put across a beauty make a smart or tricky move; eg 'Sims put across a beauty with that double dummy.' c. 1910. Mostly NZ.

put in to betray or propose; eg 'He put in word that Perkins had been seen twice in the pub during office hours.'/'He put in Perkins for the thankless job of secretary.' NZA.

put one on to punch; eg 'One more squeak out of you and I'll put one on ya.' ANZ.

put one over to deceive or outwit; eg 'You really put one over on the opposition, Snow, pretending to be limping and then suddenly streaking away for the touch down.' NZA.

put the fluence on to persuade; eg 'He respects you. If you put the fluence on, he'll join. Guarantee it.' Originally to hypnotise; c.1900, from earlier Cockney phr. for subduing or attracting. ANZ.

put the nips in/squeeze on seek to extract money or a favour; eg 'Watch out, lads, Badger's doing the rounds again putting the nips in/squeeze on.' NZA.

put up with endure or tolerate; eg 'I can barely put up with that Pom's endless whingeing.' ANZ.

put your money on guaranteed winner; eg 'You can put your money on those Labour turncoats getting another term.'

py korry by God; pidgin; eg 'Py korry, that's a good drop, eh?' NZA, and perhaps only ever in writers' minds.

Queen Street farmer
absentee landlord,
gentleman/woman farmer
rarely seen near his/her
property, which probably
tax shelter pre-
Rogernomics; in Sydney a
Pitt Street farmer, in
Melbourne a Collins Street
cockie, in Queensland a
Queen Street bushie.

queer as Chloe
homosexual, though Chloe
is who Australians were as
drunk as, with reference to
magnificent nude painting
in Melbourne hotel.

Quego Pacific Islander;
from Fijian greeting 'ko
iko', says Partridge.

quickie a fast drink/sex/
bowler in cricket; eg 'Feel
like a quickie?' for one and
two, but for three: 'He's a
genuine quickie.' ANZ.

quizzy inquisitive to the
point of nosey parkering;
eg 'Don't be so quizzy,
Paula. It's none of your
business.' NZA.

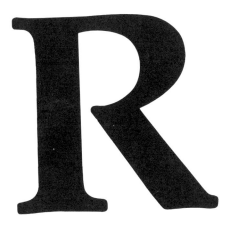

rabbiting illegal carrying of grounded rugby ball over try line. NZA.

rabid amazed or angry, or pretending so, in 1960s teen slang; eg 'Jane was rabid about losing her new Elvis record.

radical! mock horror among Yuppie types; used in satirical revue skits *Trendy Ladies* by Ginette McDonald and Sue Wilson, later by Waitemata Mayor Tim Shadbolt.

raining like a drunken dog raining heavily; variant on 'raining cats and dogs'. [*Shepard*]

rajah tumescent penis; eg 'Boy, the moment she came into the room I could feel this gi-normous rajah coming on.'

Rangitoto Yankee Aucklander, allegedly of the brash imitation American variety, equivalent of Fitzroy Yank in Melbourne, Woolloomooloo Yank in Sydney.

rapt overjoyed, short for enraptured; eg 'We were just rapt to be selected, yeh, it's a great honour, you know.' NZA.

rat steal or plunder; John A. Lee's *Civilian into Soldier*, 1937: 'There must be a lot of Huns to rat.' NZA.

ratbag troublemaker or uncouth person or engaging non-conformist; eg 'The fellow's an utter ratbag, I'd keep away if I was you.' ANZ.

rat factory psychiatric hospital; eg 'Poor Julie's been sent off to the rat factory again.'

rate of knots, a very fast; NZA and navy c.1860, but Turner says claimed for NZ; certainly popular here, where sportspeople are always going 'at a rate of knots'.

rations phr. **cut one's rations** ultimate uxorial threat to deny conjugal rights; eg 'Freddy's got a face as long as last week, the missus must have cut his rations again.'

ratshit ill or ghastly, from depression or hangover perhaps.
— broken or useless.
— no good; eg 'I feel ratshit', 'That spanner is ratshit', 'This tucker is ratshit'.
All NZA.

ratty silly, stupid or slightly eccentric; eg 'The guy's ratty.' NZA.

ratty on/ratty over infatuated; eg 'He's ratty over Mildred.' NZ late C19, Australia later.

rearend loader active male homosexual.

reck a bad thing; eg 'That stuff you got off Sibby, I tried it, it's reck, eh.' [*Alison Gray*]

Red Fed member of the Federation of Labour, perceived as a Communist agitator by conservatives or cynical seekers of political advantage. Originally really was Red, the first Federation of Labour founded 1908 by miners and other small unions and affiliated to international socialist movement. Also Australia.

Remmers Remuera, in the trendy nickname Remuera-ites have given what they regard as Auckland's — and New Zealand's — most exclusive suburb.

rigger quart of beer, precursor of the half-gallon jar; short for 'squarerigger'.

right secure state philosophically important to traditional Kiwi person; **I'll see you right** reassurance that hospitality or a loan will be extended; **she's right/ she'll be right/she's jake/ she's apples/she's sweet/ too right** all emphasising that all is secure and settled. NZA.

right as a daisy all is well; local variant of many 'right as . . .' colloquialisms like 'right as rain', denoting security or safety. [*Shepard*]

ringbolt stowaway, with crew connivance.

rip into attack with fists or words, often in positive fashion, such as aiming to move a pile of rubble; eg 'Let's rip into this digging of the swimming pool, should only take us a few hours.' NZA.

ripper! excellent; eg 'Got tickets for the game? You have? Ripper!' NZA.

rip shit and bust a big effort, often sporting; also **rip split or bust**; eg 'Okay, team. If we're to have any chance of pegging this game back in the second half, it's got to be rip, shit and bust!' NZA.

roadroller bushman or hick; early C20.

Roaring Meg a raging river, perhaps near a Gentle Annie mountain; possibly after legendary Irish landlady Maggie (Mag or Meg) Brennan of the Queenstown area who allegedly bellowed at customers and threw stroppy clients in the nearby creek; ref. James McNeish's *Tavern in the Town*; also the name of a Londonderry gun.

rock chopper Roman Catholic (after initials?). ANZ.

rock college prison. NZA.

rod walloper male masturbator. NZA.

Rogernomics the freeing up of the New Zealand economy by Roger Douglas, Minister of Finance since 1984.

rooster a person, a genial usage often qualified by 'old' or 'odd'; eg Gordon Slatter's *A Gun in My Hand*: 'He's not a bad sorta rooster.'

root, hog or die slogan of pioneering resolve. [*Jim Henderson*]

root more, eat more, drink more piss informal chant of the NZ police Red Squad prominent in control of crowds protesting 1981 Springbok tour here; NZ *Listener*, 22 August 1981, underlined the acronym: '*R*oot more, *E*at more. *D*rink more piss. Red, Red, Red. Red's the best.' Popular with rednecks and others thereafter, as macho drinking chant.

root my boot! exclamation of astonishment or disbelief, eg 'You're sure he's a shirt lifter? Well, root my boot, I'd never have picked it.'

rooted exhausted, not necessarily from sexual activity; eg 'That second half really took it out of me. I'm rooted!' NZA.

rooter active heterosexual. NZA.

root-faced humourless. NZA.

rootrat active heterosexual.

ropeable very angry; from need to rope up a difficult beast; eg 'Their coach after the game was ropeable!' NZA.

rough spin unlucky period, aka **rough trot**; eg 'Mac's had a rough spin of late.'
— **a bit rough** unfair; eg 'He wants full payment now. That's a bit rough.'

rough as guts crude, inferior, very rough; eg 'This car is as rough as guts. Needs servicing, for sure.' NZA.

round the world for threepence/fourpence/ninepence drinking methylated spirits: reinforced by Jim Henderson's memorable description of his one snort of meths, mistaken for cough mixture, as 'utterly vile, then chest lit up like a cauliflower'.

rousie rouseabout or shearing shed hand. ANZ.

rubbidy pub, rhyming slang 'rub-a-dub/pub'; aka **rubbity, rubbidy-dub, rubberdy** and **rubby**. ANZ.

rubbish to dismiss, criticise harshly or tease; eg 'I wouldn't rubbish him just yet, he could still come good.' NZA c.1925, Brit. later.

rubydazzler excellent person or thing, a rube for short; variant of Brit. 'bobbydazzler'; eg 'All those scones, for how many of you ratbags! That Noeline's a rubydazzler, and I hope you appreciate it.' NZA.

rugger bugger perfervid rugby supporter. NZA.

rumty excellent person or thing; contraction of 'rum-ti-tum', an English expansion of 'rum', excellent. NZA.

run like a hairy goat very slow or very fast; often of racehorse; eg Gordon Slatter's *A Gun in My Hand*: 'It ran like a hairy goat an I did me chips [money].' NZA.

run past someone present work for assessment or opinion; eg 'I'd like to run these figures past you one more time, okay?'

rust bucket old car. NZA.

ruth vomit, phr. **cry ruth**; derived from the sound involved. NZA.

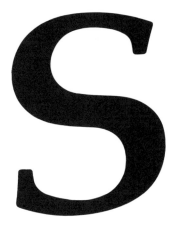

sailer loose branch; New Zealand forestry term for what wind does.

sale to vomit; often **make a sale**.

salubrious good weather, mostly among trampers, for whom **salubing** is sunbathing and a **salubrium** is a rest in the sun.

salvage scrounge or steal; WWI Anzacs, later general.

Sami Samoan; originally prison use.

sandwich short of a picnic, a a brick short of a load.

Sandy Hookers people from Nelson; after Farewell Spit.

s'arvo this afternoon; eg 'See you s'arvo.' NZA.

savs and pavs saveloys and pavlova cake, the traditional Kiwi party fare.

save a match and buy a farm be frugal; used 1920s — early 1930s, says Jim Henderson.

scale disappear quickly or furtively, to steal or rob; originally from scaling a ride on trams or trains, or taking a free ride. ANZ.

scaler robber, especially from his mates; c.1920. ANZ.

scaly bloke thin man, c.1935. NZA.

schlong penis; possibly cod Yiddish.

schooner 12 ounce glass of beer once popular particularly on West Coast.

scone head, or hit somebody on the head, usually its top; eg Ian Cross's *The God Boy*, 1958: 'Joe was worried in case he had really sconed the girl.' Possibly corruption of old English word 'sconce', head.
— **do one's scone** lose one's temper;
— **use your scone** advice to be sensible;
— **off one's scone** mad. All c.1935, NZA.

scone hot very good; perhaps euphemism for 'shit hot', though hot scones are very good indeed; eg 'That new batsman is scone hot!'

scratch cat sour-tempered female; c.1910.

screwy crazy; perhaps from phr. 'have a screw loose'; NZ 1910, later elsewhere.

scroggin trampers' lightweight sustaining tucker mix of raisins, sultanas, nuts, chocolate and boiled sweets; 'scrog' is Scottish and Northern English dialect for 'stunted bushes', which may or may not have transmogrified into scroggin.

scrousher old, rundown goldminer, c.1862; ref. Ruth Park's *One a Pecker, Two-a-Pecker* [Tuapeka].

scrummy lousy; WWI soldiers.

scull to drink ; eg 'I wish I hadn't sculled so much beer, it didn't do me any good. Just look at my stomach!' [*Alison Gray*]

scunge/scungy filth/filthy, eg state of some student flats, combining perhaps 'scurvy' and 'gungy'; originally used by Sydney and Melbourne university students. ANZ.

seagull casual non-union wharf labourer, often a student, accepting the scraps of work the union men did not want; made obsolete in 1970s by stiffening of union and port rules and contraction of wharf labour following containerisation.

see you in the soup, bring your own spoon ironic expectation of hard times and everybody for themselves. [*Shepard*]

seedless raisins married soldiers with no kids; in phrase of single soldiers, WWII. [*Jim Henderson*]

septic silly, self-deluded or incompetent, aka 'wanker' or wankery; from rhyming slang 'septic tank/wank'. [*Brian Sergent*]

session period of drinking in a group. ANZ and Brit.

set in a crack to settle something quickly, perhaps a wager in two-up, or to be well off or fortunate; Partridge suggests it might be from the notion of doing something as smartly as a whip is cracked; c.1890s.

set like a jelly everything okay; eg 'That mid-career move was a good one, he's set like a jelly, no worries.' [*Shepard*]

sexo used to suggest another male is well sexed, randy, ready to go sexually, often affectionately or as a greeting; in Gordon Slatter's *A Gun in My Hand*.

shag in phr. **like a shag on a rock** alone, abandoned, forlorn. NZA.

shag me! expression of astonishment and/or resignation; eg 'You say she left the country! No warning. Just like that? Well, shag me!'

shagger's back a sore back from excessive shagging or sexual intercourse or boasting that one has, to suggest sexual virility. NZA.

shag wagon/shagging wagon a van or station wagon customised for comfortable shagging or sexual intercourse. NZA.

shag-nasty affectionate male salutation suggestive of active heterosexuality; originally US and Brit. slang in 1900s for unpopular man or a rascal; eg 'G'day, shagnasty, feel like a beer?'

shagroon retired whaler married to a Maori woman, recorded John Robert Godley in 1850; Morris suggests probably modification of Irish 'shaughraun', a Saxon, hence a foreigner. Obs.
    — **shagroons** Australian squatters in Canterbury, 1851-52.

shake your shirt get stuck in, as in removal of shirt the better to work; eg Gordon Slatter's *A Gun in My Hand*: 'You'll haveta shake ya shirt and get down to some hard yakker.'

shakedown temporary bed, perhaps a camp stretcher; ref. Frank S. Anthony's *Me and Gus*. NZA.

shakes alive! exclamation, variant of 'snakes alive!', the things you saw in delirium tremens. [*Shepard*]

Shaky Isles New Zealand perceived as persistently shaken by earthquakes, as presented, for instance, in a film about New Zealand made by Australian comic Barry Humphries, in which the camera shook throughout. ANZ.

shanghai child's catapult, but not the forked stick variety, instead an inner tyre tube strip attached to a sling; Macquarie suggests a derivation from British dialect word 'shangan', a cleft stick for putting on a dog's tail; the act of shanghai-ing or press-ganging by stupefying victim, although clearly related to the East China seaport of Shanghai, has related merit for the impact of a child's shanghai; c.1902. NZA.

shark 'n' taties fish and chips.

she a substitute for 'it' in a variety of phrases intended to soothe, such as 'she'll be right' and 'she's jake'. NZA.

she didn't leave a fucking oat horse racing c/p for a filly the day after winning a race, indicating how well she came through it.

she ate up real good horse racing c/p same as above.

she wouldn't have blown out a match horse racing c/p indicating the filly finished the race without distress, breathing easily, hence fit.

sheepo shepherd. NZA.

sheila female; Macquarie suggests common Irish girl's name; Partridge traces to corruption of English dialect 'shaler'. NZA.

shelfer police informer. ANZ.

she'll be right/she's right reassuring or complacent expressions that everything is fine; eg 'She's right, mate, not to worry, we can handle anything they throw at us.' NZA.

she's apples another version of the above easygoing antipodean approach to life and its problems, not-to-worry philosophy; derived from rhyming slang 'apples and spice/nice', with perhaps the notion of apple pie order also; **she's sweet** a similar c/p. Both ANZ.

she's jake yet another reassuring phrase, indicating something is in good working order; less commonly **she's jakerloo/jake-a-bon/tray jake**; indicates French origins of 'Jacques' for 'jack', or cod or mock French extensions of 'jack', with 'bon', good, 'tray' for 'très', very; Partridge says from 'jannock', honest or equitable. All NZA.

shepherding rugby phrase for deliberately getting between ball carrier and those trying to tackle him; originally a digger becoming a squatter, trying to keep others off land he had not dug. NZA.

she's come up real good horse racing term for a filly that has returned from a spelling and is looking good.

she's/he's found another gear sporting c/p for horse or person accelerating, often when competition appears to be at full stretch.

shickered very drunk, sometimes **shicker** or even **shick**; **on the shicker** drunk; from Yiddish 'shiker', to be drunk. NZA colloquialism.

Shicker Express, The the first tram running after 6 pm in the days of 6 o'clock pub closing.

shift/move your carcass get out of the way; eg 'Shift your carcass, will you, there's a dozen more still to get on.' c. 1920; NZA, elsewhere later.

shilling-a-month man a remittance man, paid a shilling a month working his way on the ship out. The remittance man was often the black sheep of an English family, perhaps aristocratic, banished to a colony like New Zealand to live on a modest remittance from home.

shillings in the pound dull or somewhat insane; a specified figure is given, eg 'He's only 12 shillings/bob in the pound.' C.1925.

shine good or likeable, in phrases such as 'take a shine to him'. ANZ.

shingle short, a mentally deficient. NZA.

shit a brick exclamation of annoyance and/or surprise; eg Maurice Shadbolt's *Among the Cinders*, 1965: ' "A queer thing. Something psychological." "Shit a brick," he said.' c. 1925. NZA.

shit, eh? mild, maybe ironic, astonishment; eg 'Is that so? Shit, eh?' C. 1945; NZA.

shithead contemptible person; eg 'You know, that character is an out-and-out shithead.' NZ c.1918, elsewhere later.

shitheap a mess; eg 'This is hopeless, an utter shitheap.'

shithouse lousy, wretched; eg 'Sorry I can't make it, I feel shithouse.' NZA.

shit in win easily; eg 'In his form he should shit in.' NZA.

shit sandwich male homosexual act.

shit show no chance, in phr. **not a shit show**; eg 'The poor bastard hasn't a shit show of winning and looks as if he knows it.'

shit stirrer political activist; eg 'Old Paddy's a shit stirrer from way back.' NZA.

shitty bad mood, phrs. **crack a shitty, pack a shitty, throw a shitty**; eg 'I bet you he throws a shitty now we're starting to win.' NZA.

shitty-livered ill-tempered; eg 'Watch out for Curtin, he's a shitty-livered sod. He'll do you soon as look at you.' NZA.

shivers! mild exclamation, probably euphemism for 'shit!'; eg 'Oh, shivers, I think I've broken your cup.'

shook on very keen on person or thing; eg 'I can't say I'm much shook on a guy who marches in as if he owns the place.' NZA.

shoot off/through leave suddenly or improperly; eg 'Todd, we have to shoot through, mate. Sorry, ta-ta.' NZA.

shoot one's bolt male ejaculation, often premature, or to have given one's best and/or all; eg 'Ben's shot his bolt this round.' NZA.

shot full of holes tipsy; Anzacs WWI: Kiwis 1915, Australians 1918.

shoulda shot that horse comment on bad booze, usually after first sip, especially of home brew. [*Jim Henderson*]

shouse something very bad; contraction of 'shithouse'; eg 'It's total shouse out there, why not wait until it eases, eh?' NZA.

shout to buy somebody a present, usually an alcoholic drink or treat such as a cinema ticket; probably from English habit of shouting to waiters to replenish the drinks; eg 'Isn't it your shout, Herb?' NZA.

shovel it! expression of disbelief, suggesting that bullshit is being shovelled; often accompanied by motion of shovelling imaginary bullshit; eg 'You expect me to believe that! Ahh . . . shovel it!'

show house; as in Frank S. Anthony's *Me and Gus*: 'live in one show'.

shower, phr. **I didn't come down in the last shower** claim to be not gullible, but shrewder than given credit for. NZA.

shrapnel small change; originally used WWI soldiers of French small currency notes that were worn full of holes as if hit by shrapnel.

shrewd head/shrewdie a shrewd person, the latter applying also to a shrewd trick, in phr. **pull a shrewdie**; eg 'If you're going to play poker with him be on your guard, for sure he'll pull a shrewdie.' NZA.

shunt dismissal; eg 'Well, Ma, I got the shunt today.' NZA.
— copulation; eg 'Gave her a quick shunt and then I was off like a robber's dog.'

shypoo inferior booze, as once sold in a sly grog shop known as a 'shypoo shanty', from Cantonese 'sai po', little shop. NZA.

sickie a day off work, allegedly because ill; c.1930. NZA.

silly as a wet hen than which little comes sillier.

sink drink alcohol, often in matey phr. **sink a few beers**. NZA.

sit up like Jacky to behave at one's best, or confidently; Jacky being a common name for many people and things; the origins are uncertain, but the common name for an organ grinder's monkey is likely; c. 1930. NZA.

six o'clock swill rapid male drinking in male-only public bars in the lead-up to 6 pm pub closing time, usually from end of work at 5 pm. Perceived as piggish and the closest we got to a direct connection between beer hoses and customers. The practice ended in New South Wales after 39 years in 1955, New Zealand finally following suit when we voted, on 23 September 1967, to extend hotel opening hours. NZA.

sixpence worth of God help me waiting at the chemist's door for relief said of somebody looking seedy, in need of a pick-me-up, pre-WWII. [*Shepard*]

skate phr. **do a skate** to disappear hurriedly; aka **skate off**; eg 'Potts figured there was trouble brewing and did a skate.' c. 1925.
— phr. **go for a skate** a fall, mistake, failure, blunder or dismissal; eg 'If he doesn't shape up soon he'll go for a skate.'
— **skate over/around** to avoid, move over or blur

something disconcerting; eg 'She's always skating around the question, never really answering directly.' NZA.

skerrick small amount of money, in phr. **not a skerrick**; from Yorkshire dialect word for a fragment or particle; eg 'Sorry, mate, can't afford a ticket this week, I haven't got a skerrick on me.' NZA.

skin a rabbit undress a child. [*Shepard*]

skinful large amount of alcohol imbibed; if you have **had a skinful**, you are drunk; eg 'Aw, yeh, you got me this time, ossifer. I've had a skinful.' NZA.

skinner broke or empty; in latter case you might say 'the beer's a skinner'.

skite boaster; abbreviation of 'blatherskite', Northern and Scottish dialect 'skyte'.
— a dog foolishly capering about in front of sheep.
— **skitey** boastful; c.1925. NZA.

skizziest very good; 1960s teen slang, usually girls; ref. Jim and Mary Barr research for TVNZ series *Peppermint Twist*.

slabby timber worker handling slabs of timber; eg G.B. Lancaster's *Tracks We Tread*, 1907: 'The clumsiest slabby that lumped in the mill.'

slap-up battle or attack; WWI soldiers.

slatie a slater or woodlouse; juvenile word; 'slater' Scottish/Northern English, part of Scotland/ Otago pioneer connection.

sleep in the star hotel open-air slumber under a clear sky, in tramps' words, c.1932.

sleep with Mrs Green open-air slumber in tramp parlance, c.1932.

sling it in resign, abandon, give up; eg 'If the job's getting you down, why not just sling it in?' NZA.

slinter, sometimes **slanter**, occasionally **shlanter**, a trick; adapted from 'schlenter' or 'slenter', probably Afrikaans or Dutch for an untrustworthy person on South African diamond fields; eg Gordon Slatter's *A Gun in My Hand*: 'Wilkinson . . . worked a slinter at the end.'

slutdust household dust swept under bed or carpet.

sly grog selling grog illicitly, usually after closing time, and thus compulsively popular in era of the six o'clock swill, but goes back to our beginnings, indeed to 1829 in Australia.

slyballs derogatory term for a male; eg 'Carpy's a real slyballs, eh?' [*Alison Gray*]

smacker mouth, perhaps by association with smacking of lips.
— a lad, who may be smacked.
NZA.

smackers/smackeroos dollars, previously pounds sterling, from the South American English 'smacker', a peso, which became US for dollar, perhaps helped by sound a silver dollar made hitting the counter. NZA mostly, also Brit.

smack-up a fight, c.1906; a battle in WWI; later used Australia.

smeller objectionable fellow; from smell; eg G.B. Lancaster's *Sons o' Men*, 1904: 'Walt, you are a smeller.' Late C19. [*Partridge*]

smoke, phr. **go into smoke** go into hiding, disappear. ANZ.

smoking codfish exclamation of surprise and concern; a Shepard example: 'Smoking codfish, you're not going to take the car through that, are you? You'll get stuck!'

smoko tea-break; c.1900. NZA.

smoothieboots/ smoothiechops a ladies' man, extensions of smoothie; perhaps Dutch 'smutte', to slink, dialect English 'smoot', to creep, 'smoot after', to court a girl surreptitiously.

smoothiepuss a pretty woman. (Also 'smoothy'.)

smooze local variant of Australian 'smoodge', to kiss and cuddle, or ingratiate oneself, from Yiddish 'schmooze' and/or Southern English 'smudge', both to caress, dialect word 'smouch', whence American 'smooching', kissing and cuddling.

snag sausage. NZA.
— **a few snags short at the barbie** not quite right in the head; army.

snare seize, win; from snaring animals; eg 'How about we raid their drinks cabinet and snare a few and shoot through, eh?' NZA.

snarf gobble up or snaffle food. [*Leland*]

snark off to be miffed; colloquialism encountered recently by author in Auckland.

snarler sausage; perhaps adapted from 'snarl(e)y goster', Royal Navy slang for sausage.

snig to drag a heavy load with ropes and chains; originally logging word for dragging a log.
— **snigged home** tied up, pulled into place, piled up, as in Frank S. Anthony's *Me and Gus*; Barry Crump in *Hang on a Minute, Mate* refers to a **snigging track**; origins obscure, Northern English dialect word. NZA.

snitcher attractive person or thing, c.1935. NZA.

snitch on feeling of ill will; eg Gordon Slatter in *The Pagan Game*: 'The selector had a snitch on me.' NZA.

snodger first rate; popular with juveniles between two world wars. NZA.

snork baby; corruption of 'stork', the alleged bearer of babies. NZA.

snozzler any truly excellent person or thing; possibly a blend of 'snifter', a fine person or thing, and 'bobbydazzler'; c.1935.

sook/sookie timid person, crybaby; from 'sukey', a servant, an English lower class name for 'Susan', which was a frequent name for a servant; eg 'Martha, don't be such a sook, Sammy didn't hurt you really.' NZA.

sool set a dog on somebody; from 'sowl', English dialect word meaning to handle roughly; eg 'If you jokers don't clear off I'll sool the dog on ya.' NZA.

sooner a horse jibbing, one that would sooner go back than forward, a lazy horse — or person. NZA.

spanker cow turd, particularly useful, when dried out, as a juvenile missile; recorded use even in inner Wellington pre-WWII, author's *In Praise of Older Buildings*. NZA.

sour grape rape; eg 'He got seven years for sour grape.' Underworld.

spannerhead electrical or mechanical engineer; army slang.

spew, phr. **have a spew** big emotional outpouring. [*Alison Gray*]

spoil stolen property; c.1932, according to Partridge.

spot $100 bill, formerly £100 bill, popular among poker players; linked with 'spot', to gamble; NZA. — to pick out the best land for farm or station; c.1898.

spud potato, as recorded by Edward Jerningham Wakefield as whaling slang here in *Adventure in New Zealand*, 1845, some years before recorded in English usage; possibly derived from three-pronged digging fork.

Square Dinks First Battalion, NZ Rifle Brigade, WWI, from shoulder flash.

squarerigger half-gallon jar of beer, named after gin bottles recycled for beer pre-WWII; **Squarerigger Gully** a working class inner suburb of Wellington so called because of men coming home from the pub up Aro Street with their squareriggers of beer; recorded in author's *In Praise of Older Buildings.*

squat to run stock without permission. NZA.

squattocracy wealthy landowners who assume aristocratic airs. NZA.

squeaker child; originally old whaling term.

squiz a glance, often calculating, combining squint and quiz; eg 'Take a squiz at that upstairs window on the right, Clem. I think somebody's spying on us.' NZA.

starter somebody ready for anything; eg 'I'm a starter for a pub crawl.' NZA mostly.

staunch drunk and/or stroppy; eg staunch on whisky. [*Alison Gray*]

steal the show unexpected star of the show, often ahead of better known performers; first recorded, says Partridge, by *New Zealand Freelance* of 24 August 1934, of British batsmen to an Australian bowler in cricket match: 'It seems we've stolen the show, Aussie.' NZA and elsewhere.

steel beak shearing shed hand; from shears.

steinie a Steinlager brand of beer.

stick through provide somebody with a telephone connection; eg 'Hold on two ticks, dearie, and I'll stick you through.'

stick up to delay, hold up or bring to a standstill; used in shearing; eg 'We could do without this stick up, now we're certain to be late.'

stickybeak meddling or inquisitive person, from Australian bird getting beak sticky in search for food; eg 'Please, sir, Brenda's being a stickybeak. She's got no business peering in my desk.' ANZ.

stiff unlucky, often expressed sarcastically in such phrases as **stiff luck, stiff cheese, stiff cheddar**; eg 'I've just eaten the last sausage roll. Stiff cheese, old boy. Teach you to be late.' NZA.

stiffen the crows! exclamation of surprise and/or shock; a Shepard use was when chancing upon a wallet of notes in the back of the Matukituki. ANZ.

stipe stipendiary racecourse steward. NZA.

stir shit out of to scold comprehensively; eg 'If he doesn't buck his ideas up smartly, I am going to cheerfully stir shit out of him.' c. 1940.

stir the porridge one of the last turns in a gang rape. NZA.

stir the pot incite trouble, often politically; eg 'Old Banksy's always stirring the pot when it comes to mining rights.'

stirrer troublemaker, especially in politics; eg 'Parkin, gentlemen, is just your typical union stirrer, kneejerk demands every time he opens his agricultural mouth.' NZA.

stone ginger a certainty; eg 'Pigmy Pride is a stone ginger for the Great Hurdles.' c. 1910.

stonkered exhausted, outwitted, defeated, drunk — any or all of these; WWI use as 'out of action'; eg 'Chaps, go on without me, I'm stonkered.' NZA.

stop off to cease; eg 'Stop off, will you. Can't you see the fellow's about to cark?' c. 1880.

stoush fight; from dialect word 'stashie' or 'stushie', a quarrel; in WWI artillery bombardment was 'the big stoush'. NZA.

straight off the turnips country bumpkin; originally Yorkshire; eg 'That lad on the woolpress is hopeless, must be straight off the turnips.' c. 1932.

straight wire, the the truth, genuine news; eg G.B. Lancaster's *Sons o' Men*, 1904: 'Walt, you are a smeller, straight wire.' NZA.

streak tall thin person, often in phr. **a streak of weasel piss**. NZA.

strength of it, the reliable information or the extent of something under discussion, often as **that's about the strength of it**; used by Charles Money in *Knocking About in New Zealand*, 1871.

stretcher case sporting injury, or somebody who stoically and rashly plays on with an incapacitating injury; NZA.
— somebody peculiar or eccentric enough to be carted away on a stretcher, to a mental asylum.

strife trouble, often in phrs **more strife than a pork chop in a synagogue/ than a pregnant nun**. NZA.

strike me handsome! well, fancy that! Variant of strike me lucky/pink. [*Shepard*]

string along to deceive; eg 'You could string him along a bit more, he looks pretty gullible.' c. 1920. Mostly NZ.

stripy streaky, unconvincing, variable; late C19.

stuff to defeat severely, often in sport; c.1920; in phr. **not give a stuff** not to care; eg 'Nobody gives a stuff about the score, it's the game that counts with us.' Mostly NZA.

stuff and butter me! for goodness sake!; army; eg 'Not another ruddy underage recruit. Stuff and butter me! Can't you read birth certificates?'

stuff off! a strong request to leave; eg 'Look, mate, nobody asked you to this party. Now why don't you stuff off before we have to call the police?'

stuff it! exclamation of frustration, probably anger too; eg 'Stuff it! That's the umpteenth time I've just missed the bull.' NZA.

stuffed exhausted, ruined, dead drunk; eg 'I'm utterly stuffed. I'll have to flag this marathon lark away.' NZA.

stumered bankrupt or exhausted; from English use of 'stumer', a dud cheque; **come a stumer** a fall, usually financial; **in a stumer** in a mess, usually financial; eg 'I'm stumered, mate, you're on your own the rest of this match.' NZA.

stunned drunk; eg 'Can't you see he's stunned? He's been boozing since the pubs opened.' c. 1910, Australia and elsewhere later.

suff enough; short for sufficient; eg G.B. Lancaster's *Sons o' Men*, 1904: 'I've 'ad suff o' you, Tommy. I'm goin' 'ome.' From c.1880.

Sunday dog lazy sheep or cattle dog. NZA.

supersnagative first rate; eg 'I didn't know you made pin cushions. That detail is lovely. Supersnagative.' c. 1890. NZA.

swag informal backpack of stroller-after-work; hence **swagman**, the tramp or stroller carrying a swag; also **swaggie**; NZA.

— **go on the swag** become a tramp; NZA.

— **a swag of** a lot of; re-emergence of early C19 c/p c.1930.

— **look for one's swag-straps** consider looking for another job.

swannie large woollen bush shirt-cum-coat; from Swanndri brand name.

swept cleaned out of money; WWI soldiers.

swerve avoidance of something disagreeable; eg 'I'll give the party a swerve.'

swi/swy two-up gambling game involving the betting on how two tossed coins will land; from German 'zwei', two; c.1920. ANZ.

swiftie trick or deception, usually in phr. **pull/work a swiftie**; eg 'Brendan's ducked off from taking a leak and it's his shout. Looks like he's pulled another swiftie on us.' ANZ.

swing the gate fastest shearer in the shed. NZA.

taihoa wait! Hang on a minute, mate; Williams translates as 'by and by'.

taipo dark dog; Kiwi colloquialism from mid-C19 and extant (Ref. guard dog at Fyffe House, Kaikoura); or a vicious horse.
— Maori slang for a theodolite, a land-stealing devil or goblin; confused origins, with Bennett suggesting a Maori word which Pakeha assumed meant a devil; Williams says it is a word used by the Maori believing it English, and by the English believing it Maori, when it is apparently neither.

tails batmen serving with high ranks, WWI soldiers; perceived as the opposite of heads, in the head and tail sides of the coin in the game 'two-up'.

Takapuna surprise steak stuffed with oysters.

take out the back teeth neutering the domestic tomcat.

take the day off to carry bricks a working holiday.

takey-ah-ways take-away food, pronounced as if a Maori word.

talk a glass eye to sleep boring; ref. Stevan Eldred-Grigg, *Oracles and Miracles*.

talk bullock bad language bullock drivers were noted for; ref. Sam under 'bullocky'.

talk the leg off an iron pot you talk too much. NZA.

Taranaki cow any nondescript or poorly conditioned cow.

Taranaki exquisite nickname for person from Taranaki in provincial government times.

Taranaki gate any home-made gate of wire and wood for corralling livestock.

Taranaki topdressing cow dung.

Tararua dishmop *Raouli tenuicaulis* plant, used by trampers to clean out pots and billies. (Cf mountain mop.)

technicolour yawn vomit. ANZ.

ten bob to a nob of goatshit a confident or odds-on avowal; eg 'Ten bob to a nob of goatshit he can't run a full marathon.'

Terries, the Territorial Army; ref. Partridge and Gordon Slatter; c. 1930.

that'll be the day c/p expressing doubt or incredulity; NZ since 1930s, widespread elsewhere; also, **that'll be the bloody day, boy!**

that'll be the frosty Friday/frozen fortnight Kiwi variants of 'that'll be the day', which Partridge thinks derives from WWI officer usage.

that's a bit hot! a protest against something unreasonable; eg 'C'mon, Perce, that's a bit hot, no need for that sort of language. There's ladies present, in case you hadn't noticed.' c. 1910. NZA.

that's borer dust that's a lot of nonsense or rubbish. [*Shepard*]

that's our muttons just what we like, with reference to the excellence of our mutton; eg 'Look at our rowing eight go. That's our muttons!' NZA.

they must have captured a sugar boat WWI soldiers' reaction to receiving a generous sugar ration.

they're off, Mr Cutts the race has begun; Partridge identifies as a variant of '"they're off," said the monkey', usually indicating start of a horse race, hence as something that has come loose; often with addition: 'when he looked into the lawnmower and carelessly lost his testicles'.

This addition may explain Mr Cutts. NZA.

tickets on oneself, have to be conceited; eg 'That stuck-up bastard, he's got tickets on himself.' NZA.

tickle to steal or rob, often in phr. **to tickle the peter**, to rob the till; NZ c.1932, Australia later.

tiffin midmorning cuppa and snack, late C19; from Anglo-Indian word for a light lunch. [*Partridge*]

tight as a duck's arse, also **bull's/gnat's/fish's** mean with money; often carrying the response: **and that's water tight**. NZA.

tin arse lucky person; also **tinbum**; eg 'First time he's ever swung a golf club and he scores a hole in one. What a tin arse!' NZA.

tin can old and noisy motorcar, often 'tin-can on wheels'. NZA mostly.

tin canning a greeting, often of newly-weds, by tin can bashing, often now for sport or rock music performers; originally and still occasionally aka **tin kettling**. NZA.

tinny lucky, possibly by association with English 'tinny', rich; eg 'The ball just hit his racket and dobbed over the net. How tinny can you get!' NZA. — not very impressive; from tin being regarded as an inferior metal to iron or steel; eg 'I tell you that horse is tinny, it'll never amount to anything.'

titoki a beer/lemonade/ raspberry shandy (gaff), from its similarity to titoki berry juice. [*Acland*]

ti-tree oneself take shelter from artillery bombardment, WWI; perhaps recalling Maori going ti-tree or bush so successfully in the land wars; ref. James Belich's *The New Zealand Wars* p.317 for Maori trench warfare techniques perhaps taught to British officers before WWI.

tizzy up dress up for an outing; probably derived from 'titivate'; eg 'Well, ladies, are you going to go and tizzy up before we leave?' NZA.

toe-ragger swagman, down-and-outer, nowadays usually 'toerag', a term of affectionate abuse; probably from the foot-bindings tramps or swaggies wore; the whalers used **toe-riggers** as a term of abuse, probably derived from Maori 'taurekareka', a contemptuous term for a slave or captive taken in war.

toey anxious, randy, ready, excitable; originally of a keen sprinter in horse racing; eg 'Am I toey tonight! I must score or I'll go apeshit.' NZA.

togs swimming trunks for football gear; contracting English meaning of any clothes. NZA.

toity toilet, often **down the toity** to lose something, or fail; eg 'There goes another Lotto ticket down the toity.'

tonguing perming hair in electrically heated rollers; ref. Stevan Eldred-Grigg's *Oracles and Miracles*.

tonky fashionable; possible blend of 'toney' and 'swanky'; eg 'My, my, doesn't she look tonky.' c. 1935.

touch somebody's turn to buy a round of drinks; eg 'Hey, Sid, isn't it your touch?'

touch your kick a modest loan, a 'kick' being old word for sixpence; common request by Pedlar Thomas quoted NZ Oral History Unit Martinborough study.

Triangle Dinks Third Battalion, NZ Rifle Brigade, WWI, from shoulder flash.

trick an amusing or alert child; eg 'Now isn't little Katie a trick.' NZA.

tripe human intestines in phrs **I'll tear your tripes out** an exaggerated threat of a thrashing, usually to badly behaved juvenile; **don't bust your tripe** don't overdo it.

tripehound sheepdog. NZA.

trol female; short for trollop, but less particular or offensive.

troppo displaying mental unsteadiness, often in phr. **gone troppo**; Anzac word for WWII Pacific theatre servicemen too long in the tropics and badly in need of repatriation. ANZ.

trot luck, usually in 'bad trot' or 'good trot', mostly sport use; probably from two-up game, where a trot is a sequence of heads; eg 'It's ages since I had a decent trot.'
— **on the trot** a sequence, often a winning one, more usually picking a succession of horse race winners nowadays.
— **do a trot** have a good run of luck. All NZA.

trot a woman, perhaps desired, as used by Gordon Slatter; probably a lightening of English word 'trot', whore; c.1925.

trots race meeting for (horse) trotters. NZA.

truesville very true; an example of American-influenced 1960s teens adding 'ville'.

trump of the dump anyone in authority; WWI.

tucker food; originally rations on the gold diggings; probably from the act of tucking in or eating heartily.
— **earn your tucker** working for board and lodgings; eg 'The way things are going, there won't be any casual labourers left to earn their tucker.' ANZ mostly.

tucker fucker army cook.

tug to masturbate. NZA

turd burglar male homosexual.

turkey will roost on your lip, a a warning to a youngster not to pout or sulk. [Jean Henderson]

turkey off absent without leave; WWI. NZA.

turn it on give a party or buy drinks; eg 'What do you say we turn it on for the boys tonight?' NZA.

turn it up make oneself, usually a female, available for sex; eg 'Hey, Mort, reckon that sheila over there'd turn it up?'

turn Nagasaki become nasty as when atom bomb struck Nagasaki; eg 'No need to turn Nagasaki on me, mate. I'm on your side.' Underworld.

turn-out gathering of people, from English specific meaning of voters going to polls; eg 'Not a bad turn-out for Housie considering the weather.'
— mode of transport, such as a bike or side-car; as recorded in Frank S. Anthony's *Me and Gus*.

turps any alcohol; **on the turps** on a drinking bout. NZA.

tussock jumper station hand.

tussocker shearer or casual labourer arriving at dusk to avoid work but not the tucker; from his tussock grass hide; 'sundowner' in Australia.

twin-set and pearls set comfortable middle-class conservative antipodean ladies identified from clothing; 'twin-set' recorded in America in 1937.

two bastards on bikes reaction of those betting two heads when two tails are tossed in gambling game 'two-up'; **two ladies on bikes** if betting tails.

two shakes of a dog's hind leg give me a few seconds and I'll be with you; variant **two shakes of a dead lamb's tail** rather less basic. NZA.

two-thirds of five-eighths of fuck all very little; eg 'What did you make at the races?' 'Two-thirds of five-eighths of fuck all.' From the end line of the limerick:
There was a young man from Bengal
Who had an elliptical ball.
The square root of his prick
Time seven-eighths of his grip
Was two-thirds of five-eighths of fuck all.

tyke Catholic; Partridge says variant of 'Teague', Ulster name for Roman Catholic, originally English transcription of Irish name 'Tadhg', an Irishman. ANZ.

unbutton the mutton to urinate; eg 'Scuse I while I just go and unbutton the mutton.' ANZ.

underdungas underpants, possibly from dungas as short for dungarees. Mostly NZA.

underground mutton rabbit. NZA.

uni contraction of university. Mostly NZA.

up large drinking heavily and/or heartily, contraction of 'piss up large'; eg 'Okay, now the woofters have gone, let's all up large, eh?'

up shit creek in leaky gumboots in trouble; variant on being up shit creek without a paddle. [*Jim Henderson*]

up the chute worthless, stupid, wrong; eg 'Sorry, chum, you're up the chute on that one.' NZA.

up the Cook's hooray! May you flourish; army c/p of encouragement; linked by Partridge to names of regiments. [*Jim Henderson*]

up the Dutch shit in trouble; eg 'Are we up the Dutch shit with this batch!'

up the Mokau up the creek or up the boohai; from a remote North Taranaki river; eg 'You jokers are up the Mokau with that notion.'

up the wop pregnant.
— broken, not functioning;
eg 'That doll's house
you've built is totally up
the wop.'
NZA.

**useless as a tit on a hand/
as a gumdigger's dog**
very useless; eg 'I hate to
say this, but when it comes
to gardening, you're as
useless as a tit on a hand/
as a gumdigger's dog.'

ute utility van or small
truck, contraction;
originally WWII, mostly
NZA.

vegemite a good child or an amused term for a child; eg 'What a little ookycooky vegemite you are, yes you are.' ANZ.

vegetable go to sleep or look dazed; street talk; eg 'Foss goes vegetable on us all the time these days. [*Alison Gray*]

vegetable sheep South Island high country plant resembling resting sheep.

vertical drinking standing room only drinking in some pubs in the good old, bad old days.

vomit-making something unpleasant, such as a hideous bureaucratic paint job on a building. NZA.

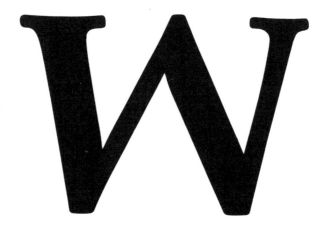

wacky baccy marijuana; variant of US drug culture 'wacky tabacky'.

waddy piece of wood; Baker suggests possibly pidgin Maori for 'wood' as well as pidgin Aboriginal for 'club'.

Wadestown wadical Yuppie (young urban professional) inhabitant of inner Wellington hill suburb of Wadestown, supposedly representing the Labour Party's trendy lefties (left wingers), slighting in suggestion of lisp.

wahine woman, often desired or seen as girlfriend or wife; from Maori, colloquialism late C19.

waipiro strong alcohol; Maori 'wai', water, and 'piro', stinking.

Waikikamukau imaginary archetypal Kiwi back-of-beyond village, with variant spellings, including **Waikikamookau** and **Waikukumukau**, former used by Minhinnick in 1920s humorous newspaper articles, the latter used by English writer Austin Mitchell in his 1972 *The Half-Gallon, Quarter-Acre Pavlova Paradise*. Becoming unacceptable in recent years, though school playgrounds may yet ask 'Waikikamukau?' and answer, 'Because it kicked me.'

Waiouru blonde sheep near army training quarters.

Waiouru limp a limp allegedly acquired in pursuit of preceding, allegedly for sexual purposes.

waka blonde a Maori woman; offensive.

wake it up! get on with it! eg 'Wake it up, will you, we haven't got all day to do this.' NZA.

wake up to someone/ something recognise something has been going on, perhaps that you have been conned or tricked; eg 'It's about time you woke up to his ways. He's taking you for a ride.' NZA.

wake up to oneself recognise your own deficiency, start accepting responsibility for your actions; eg 'Wake up to yourself. You're a mess, you look like you've been through the wringer backwards.'

wattie a Pakeha attempt at 'whata', Maori for storehouse; **futtah** ditto.

weak as nun's piss very weak, often a reference to beer.

weights, phr. **putting your weights up** putting someone in trouble; possibly from weights carried in handicap horse races; eg 'I'd watch Monk if I was you, he'd put your weights up with the cops soon as look at you.' Australian miners c.1925. ANZ.

weka a Chatham Islander; used by Islanders themselves, being proud of their weka population.

well gone hopelessly in love; eg 'Cindy's well gone on old Jools, who'd have thought it, eh?' c. 1913, Australia later.
— severely wounded; WWI.

well, what do you know? mild, rhetorical, mock incredulity; eg 'Well, what do you know if it ain't old Sumpoil himself. Can't keep away from the trough, eh?' c. 1920, elsewhere later.

Wellington swell nickname for person from Wellington in provincial times.

welter, phr. **make a welter of it** to overindulge or go to extremes; early C20. NZA.

were you born in a tent? sarcastic question of somebody who has left the door open and let draughts in. NZA.

wetboot man bureaucrat, as identified within the outdoor ranks of New Zealand forestry and wildlife staff.

whacker wanker or masturbator, used as term of abuse, affection or affectionate abuse; or dismissive of a fool or idiot; from 'whack off', to masturbate, not the first antipodean or American variant of an English word for coition.

whaddarya? rhetorically questioned contempt; ref. Greg McGee's play *Foreskin's Lament*.

wharfie waterside worker. NZA.

what's that got to do with the price of eggs? challenging the relevance of some remark; Australians prefer 'fish' to 'eggs'.

when you were now, if you see what I mean when you work it out (you will know what this typically arsy-versy bit of backcountry Kiwi means). [*Shepard*]

whingeing Pom any British immigrant complaining about life here; a stereotype of the British immigrant. NZA.

whiny given to whining; NZ colloquialism late C19.

whip, phr. **crack the whip** urge to greater effort, as a jockey would; NZA.
— **fair crack of the whip** appeal for fair treatment; NZA.
— **where the whips are cracking** the front line in battle, WWI, from cattle mustering and small arms fire eliciting similar sounds.
— **whip the cat** to moan or reproach yourself; make a fuss. NZA.

whips plenty of; eg Roderick Finlayson's *Tidal Creek*, 1948: 'Got whips of land.'

white Maori tungstate of lime, among miners, c.1875.
— Maori who has adopted Pakeha name and/or ways, as quoted in New Zealand Oral History Unit study of Martinborough.

whitebaiter Maori activist; of academic origin, pun on popular seasonal fry fishers.

white-haired boy darling or favourite, antipodean variant of 'white-headed boy', with reference to the fair hair of babies.
— **you must have white hairs** said to somebody receiving an unexpected favour. [*Partridge*]

whizler a complainer, combining whinger and grizzler. [*Jean Henderson*]

whooptee bang/ whooptybang making whoopee or merrymaking; common in Northland. [*Jim Henderson*]

whopcacker extravagantly approved person or thing; extension probably of 'whop' or 'wop', to excel; eg 'Couldn't have come at a better time. Thanks, mate. You're a whopcacker!' NZA.

widdykikoo to kiss and canoodle and generally carry on, says Stevan Eldred-Grigg of what he assumes came into Christchurch working class English as dialect word from elsewhere, or was coined.

widdygiddy to behave in a flighty manner; another of the 'widdy' words Stevan Eldred-Grigg came across in researching pre-WWII Christchurch working class families. Partridge identifies 'widdy' as either a widow or the gallows in dialect and low colloquial C19, the latter Scots, possibly a pun on 'widdy', a halter. However, the juvenile or even baby talk of fanciful adults seems more likely.

widgie female bodgie, defined *Sunday Chronicle* of 6 January 1952: 'girl with horse-tail hair-do and bobby socks, also playing juke-box in milk-bar'; possibly a little wilder this side of the Tasman, where bodgies and widgies were regarded as juvenile delinquents.

wigwam for a goose's bridle evasive and/or dismissive answer to question about what one is doing; variant of 'whim-wham to bridle a goose', a 'whim-wham' being any fanciful object; eg 'What's that thing you're making?' 'Oh, just a wigwam for a goose's bridle.' NZA.

Wild Cats and Tigers' Union the New Zealand Women's Christian Temperance Union, acronymically so, c.1950.

wild Irishman a thorny shrub, aka matagouri, from Maori 'tumatakuru', or speargrass.

wild Spaniard or simply 'Spaniard', speargrass, a sub-alpine herb with leaves like a Spanish dagger and a smell like celery and turpentine.

will you peek? are you giving up? Probably from the question asked in card games involving trumping. [*Shepard*]

wobbly tantrum; **throw a wobbly** have a tantrum; can apply to person or machine; eg 'Every time I ask her to do something, she goes and throws a wobbly.'

woo a kiss and cuddle and maybe more, without necessarily intending to woo or pay court to and seek everlasting love; c.1930; eg 'Had a bit of a woo with some sheila, next thing I know, it's morning and I've slept the night in the hydrangeas.'

wood have the advantage, often to **have the wood on**; as in woodchopping contests, at least from 1941; eg 'Long as his first serve is not working,

you've got the wood on him.' NZA.

wooden to hit; used by Frank S. Anthony in *Me and Gus*.
— **wooden out** to punch somebody to the floor; eg 'He took a swing at me and missed, then I woodened him out.'

wooden aspro a truncheon across the head, as encountered most often in prisons.

Woodbines Anzacs' name for British troops WWI, because they smoked the cheap Wills Woodbine cigarettes; later applied to any Englishman.

woolbug shearer, c.1890-1940; eg Jean Devanny's *The Butcher Shop*, 1926: 'The shearers, the "wool-bugs", in their dirt and grease.'

wool king a big sheep farmer. NZA.

woopknacker a hard case, variant spelling of 'whopcacker' and once more common, from c.1920; eg Gordon Slatter: ' He's a woopknacker all right.' NZA.

wopwops remote district, variant of Australian 'woopwoops', which is apparently a satirical play on Aboriginal habit of duplication of place names; eg 'I've lived too long in the wopwops to ever get used to driving over the harbour bridge.'

would you rather walk a mile and climb a stile or eat a sunburned cake? (cowpat) question for somebody objecting to walking, usually asked by parent of a child in grave danger of being left behind among the cowpats.

wouldn't call the king me uncle elation, high spirits, triumph; eg 'You see Hadlee equalling the world record? Incredible, eh? Gorh, wouldn't call the king me uncle.' [*Jim Henderson*]

wouldn't it! exclamation of disgust or exasperation; eg 'Wouldn't it make you spit tacks!' c. 1925, NZA.

wouldn't it rip your ration book/rock you/root you/rotate you/rot your socks/make you spit?/make you spit chips?' extensions of above exclamation, sometimes including being startled or unsettled, especially in 'rock' and 'rotate'; the latter recorded by Jim Henderson in his *Gunner Inglorious*, 1945; eg 'Well, did you hear about Sid winning the quinella? First time he's punted. Wouldn't it rip your rationbook/rock you/rotate you etc . . .' NZA.

wouldn't know shit from clay naive or stupid persons; eg 'Monty's so dense he wouldn't know shit from clay.'

wouldn't know the Brighton tram was up them till it rang its bell and people started getting off, preceded by 'so tight', meaning very mean with money, but could as well be used to mean slow-witted; former meaning quoted in Stevan Eldred-Grigg's *Oracles and Miracles.*

wouldn't touch it with a red-hot poker extreme aversion; eg 'If I was you I wouldn't touch those shares with a red-hot poker.' NZA.

wow mental asylum; from the Whau River next to Auckland's Oakley mental hospital; ref. Greg Newbold's *The Big Huey.*

wowser teetotaller, prude, killjoy, excessively religious; originally a prohibitionist, acronymically named by Australian political journalist John Norton 1862-1916: We Only Want Social Evils Remedied; Macquarie also suggests a link with English dialect word 'wow', to whine. Australia c.1895, NZ soon after.

wraxing swinging backwards and forwards, as on the legs of a chair, which Stevan Eldred-Grigg exemplifies thus: 'Stop that bloody wraxing on that bloody chair.'

wrung out like a dishcloth exhausted from heat or excessive activity; eg 'You haven't the foggiest, you know. After a night cleaning offices, you're wrung out like a dishcloth.'

XYZ

XYZ the YMCA, ironically displaced acronym, WWI soldiers.

XYZee! your zipper is undone!

yakker ; often **hard yakker**. Aboriginal word. ANZ.

yammer whine or complain. ANZ.

yank tank large American car. ANZ.

yecch! exclamation of disgust, variant of 'yuck!', sometimes combining intimations of vomit. NZA.

yee-ha! exclamation of exhilaration and/or approval (as entered in comments book at Rore Hapipi play *Tupuna*, at the Depot, Wellington, August, 1987). NZA.

Yellow Peril the Chinese Communists perceived by xenophobic antipodeans as imminent invaders.

yodel over the mahogany to vomit.

you can put a ring around that you can be sure of that; from ringing some item with a pencil so it stands out on the page; ref. Gordon Slatter; c. 1925.

you can't fatten thoroughbreds so I'm skinny — but I'm classy! Anyway, that's my excuse for being thin. [*Shepard*]

you could whip a cricket over it any time impoverished land; eg 'Last summer you could've whipped a cricket over that field, now look at it, covered in chest-high corn.' [*Jean Henderson*]

you get that resigned acceptance of a remark; eg 'Ah, well, with his sort you get that.'

you make a better door than a window addressed to somebody needlessly in your way, perhaps standing in front of the television; c. 1920. NZ and US.

you think you're a flowerpot because you've got a hole in your bum you fancy yourself; ref. Stevan Eldred-Grigg in *Oracles and Miracles*.

you wouldn't read about it! something that amazes; c.1935, elsewhere later.

you're a trimmer! a compliment or a curse; from English word 'trimmer', a person who literally thrashes, meaning performs vigorously. Shepard example: 'The key is stuck in the keyhole. You think you've jiggered it. Along comes your fix-it cobber and all's well. Gee, you say. You're a trimmer.' Shepard example two: 'What did you move that for? I had them in the right order. Gawd, you're a trimmer.'

zack a sixpenny coin c.1890, possibly corruption of 'six'. NZA.

zambuck St John ambulance officer; from black and white uniform likened to the black and white container of Zambuck ointment. ANZ.

zeal suggestion for the name of the post-sterling New Zealand currency, stillborn in the face of the almighty 1967 dollar.